TO TAKE A
CHANCE

TO TAKE A
CHANCE

BRENDA HANGAN

TATE PUBLISHING
AND ENTERPRISES, LLC

Published by Tate Publishing & Enterprises, LLC
127 E. Trade Center Terrace | Mustang, Oklahoma 73064 USA
1.888.361.9473 | www.tatepublishing.com

Tate Publishing is committed to excellence in the publishing industry. The company reflects the philosophy established by the founders, based on Psalm 68:11,
"The Lord gave the word and great was the company of those who published it."

Book design copyright © 2016 by Tate Publishing, LLC. All rights reserved.
Cover design by Samson Lim
Interior design by Shieldon Alcasid

Published in the United States of America

ISBN: 978-1-68254-853-0
Games / Gambling / General
16.06.10

I AM FROM a family of gamblers. Mom would say how she and her brother would play cards with their dad, and if they lost the bet (took a chance), the money would have to be paid. Of course that's the way it should be. We take chances all the time in many ways. I remember when I used to tell a cousin to come over to my house, we would hang out and play black jack. We really didn't have money or chips, so we decided that we would take a jar of pennies that I had in the house, and we would use them as if they were chips. Oh for the good old days!

I want to make sure that I say this now way before I start to tell you anything else. This is not about any one person. This is about hundreds of people. I love gambling, and because I do gamble, I take time to go to the casino. I really enjoy myself most of the time. That's the only reason to go anywhere, even the casino. You are supposed to have a good time.

I am not in any way blaming the gambling industry, not even the casinos. I like the idea of being able to gamble. Now I can stop by any one of the casinos any time of the day and take a chance any time I want. I am sure that every human being (that would be all of us) has some things that they enjoy more or less than the next guy. Gambling is only a product that is available; you can buy it or not. It's for entertainment.

It develops into a habit. We can do it whenever we want to or whenever we can fit it in. It's okay to enjoy those pleasures.

What I am being told on a regular basis from people in all walks of life is that something has gone very wrong and that people are actually acting like they are losing their minds. People are continuing to take the chance *no matter what*. What kind of fool would do that? See, there is a reason to take the chance: it is to get something in return. Once you get it, the chance that you took has been satisfied. The task has been done. As animals, we always take a chance to obtain a product.

When we take a dollar and go to a store and buy a worm, a hook, and a fishing pole, we are taking a chance that by using these items at the lake or in the pond, we will catch a fish. That is the objective: to get that fish. Now once you obtain the fish, what are you going to do with it? You should be tickled now; look at all the things that can be done. I can just reel in that big boy, keep it in something that would make sure that it stayed fresh until I could get it home to prepare it for friends, family, and or loved ones.

There are many choices, you take the fish and gut it, wash it, and put in the freezer for a rainy day, or you can get all the joy out of catching the fish and let the fish go. I guess that means that you didn't really want a fish. It may be that you just wanted to see if you could do it. Sometimes that can be a selfish act. We all have that type of feeling about the subject in our lives, and it is okay.

What is not okay is a person taking a chance always—24 hours a day, 7 days a week, 365 days a year. And when they are not doing some type of gambling, they are clearly only thinking about the next time they can take that chance again to the point that they can't deal with the everyday stuff anymore. See, in this society, we call that an addiction. I have to say that lots of people have called and told me all kinds of story about people they all love very much; you can tell that the ones telling the story are confused, and they can't figure out what is happening.

What's wrong? It seems that taking a chance is the only thing these people have decided that they care about. Maybe at this stage of life, someone needs to say out loud, "Get back in line!" like all the rest of us sheep. People who act like there is nothing to hope for, nothing to work for, or no reason to save do not care in general about anything. They are not looking at reality.

Every generation has had an electronic stage or modern technology. There was the pinball age group, and there has been the video craze, and now there is the computer obsession. With the computer, we can do any and everything, but with technology comes some demons—you know, the things in life that we sometimes can't control. As the rest of us get past the demons we have, we still care about life and the outcome of it all, taking the chance that if we eat right, groom ourselves, and get lots of rest, that when the sun come up in the morning, we will wake up breathing and happy.

I take a chance all the time. We all do. I take a chance every time I get up and get in my car to drive Monday, Wednesday, and Friday every week. I take a chance that if I make it over to the dialysis center, sit in this chair, and let the nursing staff and the doctors do what they are skilled at doing, then I will be healthy like all the other human beings. Several times, I have been able to take yet another chance to buy my airline tickets, fly around to other states to visit my son, grandson, family, and friends. Most of the chances taken were because I couldn't and wouldn't miss out on enjoyment that we had, being part of each other's lives.

Most of the time, when I am traveling, I would have a chance to stop by a casino. To me, it is all part of the vacation. A lot of times I win, and with those winnings, I pay for the things I need and have a great time. Of course I had a plan. The goal, to take the money obtained do something good with it. Once again, I don't do this all day every day. Personally I don't have time in my life to do anything always. Even now as I look down at my shoes, I can see the paint that dripped on them from me being high up on the scaffolding, painting on a 150-year-old house rather than tearing it down or just letting time and weather continue to destroy it.

When we used to take kids to the arcades to play videos, the kids would run around all over the place, jumping all over from the floor to the table, eating pizza and having soda. They'd get tokens from their parents to play video games, and they'd play for hours, really getting lots of joy out of the day. At some point, they ask for more tokens, but the adults would say, "No more tokens." Then we all would leave the arcade. The children are having a good time, but they would have so many other things to do. There is no way the parents can allow the child to stay at the arcade any longer; the child should not spend every waking hour daydreaming about only the arcade and the videos inside. The reason that I am taking out the time to talk about this subject is because now the adults are out of control; they don't want to leave the arcade and the videos. I am sure that a lot of the fact that everyone has an income, a job, some means of support, some access to money, that gives people more of an opportunity to go out and take chances with that money. It doesn't matter if you risk your money, but have a limit. I don't care what the limit is; just have one.

Several times, people have walked up to me and handed me their money, wanting me to give them change when I have been in a casino. At that point I have to explain to them that I don't work there, so I would direct them to some employee who does. After I help them, they usually say, "I am sorry that I bothered you, but you look like you are in charge. I was thinking that you work here." I guess it's just something about me that people see. Most of my life, people have given me their belongings, always their clothes. Lately I have been surprised how many people have been giving me all their treasures that they have been saving for years to give to their children and grandchildren. What they are finding is that the family members are saying that they don't want any of the stuff. It didn't matter that the parents cared so much about the items. One of the biggest concerns that I have is that when the inheritance is given to the family, friends or whomever, they are so busy only thinking about themselves and what they want so they just get rid of the belonging left to them.

People are not taking into consideration anything else. What is so unbelievable is that these are the ones that we love. We love the person who is out of control. So what do we do? Me telling someone what they should be doing is funny because I am nobody special. I don't even pretend that I am an expert about anything.

When I told friends and others that I was going to write a book about gambling, everyone said, "Do it, please!

Maybe you could say something for those who don't seem to understand what they are doing to themselves or to the future." The first thing my friends said to me when I told them that I am going to talk to people the way that they needed to be talked to, no holds barred, I was told that if I talked like we usually talk about this subject, my book would be censored. If that was done, then I wouldn't be able to reach the people who really need to hear what is being said because I know that I would use a lot of cursing words.

Maybe that's what they need! Knowing I can't do that, then I guess I better just yell as loud as I can: Get a grip! Stop! And when you can't decide if you should risk more of the money, think.

When you decide that you don't have anything to do in your life, take a minute to relax, try for a moment to remember all the goals that you have set personality, and when you get confused about your plans, go back to the beginning, back to when we were children and the adults would ask you, "What are you going to do when you grow up?" I bet you all were so proud to give them an answer. Remember how you were excited and looked forward to all the endless possibilities that the world was going to hold for you. Try to go back and find those memories of a time when you knew that everything was good and you were ready to take it all on. Also, just look at so many of the great things in life that you always loved doing before. The hours spent growing and planning to complete all the projects you have started.

Friends often tell me that I am always busy. They ask me, "When do you rest or sleep?" I get up pretty early most days, and I am doing stuff like making coffee, washing dishes, juicing fruits and veggies, cleaning or painting one or two houses that belong to a friend I planted colorful flowers around the houses and spent time making sure that the weeds are pulled. I collect the trash and take it to the dump. I love doing that; I get to check out all the items that are still in good shape that others throw away. I cook and eat some food for energy to keep up and do all the things that I need to do before the sun goes down for the evening.

People say that they are bored, even depressed, and they can't find anything to do to fulfill their hours of the day or night. See, there are long hours without anything else for them to think of but gambling. Idle hands and idled minds, and when all else fails, they go gambling. Do it at the casino. Do it in the car. Do it on the computer. Do it on the lottery or Quick Pick and spend thousands on scratcher tickets. All I would like to tell them is, when you get these thoughts, get up, look around the house, in the backyard, or wherever you are, and decide that you are going to do something else.

Even as I am taking out this time in my life to write this very small book, I have visited the casino a few times. My friends and I enjoyed a good meal at the dining cafe and get to share some of our plans with each other for the near future and what our goals are. We can only reach these goals if you work toward them. Most of the time, when I risk my cash to take a chance, luck is on my side; and lately I have been winning more than losing. That isn't the case with a lot of customers or players.

I have noticed that in the past, when you go to the casino, people would at least spend some type of quality time working on their appearance before going to gamble, like taking a shower, doing their hair, picking out fancy clothes to wear, pulling out their good jewelry, getting all dressed up for a night on the town. I can remember too many times that I was so impressed by how nice and glamorous the surroundings are and the people matched it. Now you can see that the average person that come to the casino could care less what they are wearing or what they look like. Now, I couldn't believe that people sit in front of slot machines all laid-back in the chair, with their shoes off and they have their feet propped up on the till of the slot machine. There is no question that there is more going on at that time in their minds besides just playing a game.

Once I saw a woman take off her sweater and drape it over her head like an Indian headdress. It was as if she believed at that moment that if she was dressed in her native way of her country, then the machine would hit a jackpot and pay her. She was actually playing two slot machines. She did get one of the machines to hit a jackpot; it paid her $1,500, but while she was waiting for the casino employee to bring her winning back to her after checking with IRS for taxes that may have to be paid and recorded in her name and ID, she continued to play on the other machine. She was betting $3 at a time just like she had been doing all along on the first slot machine; she won another jackpot of $800 on the second machine; now she had a credit of money on that slot machine, she continued to play on the $800 winnings from the second machine. In the time it took for the checker to return with the money to pay her off, the woman had pushed the spin button on the second slot machine enough times that the money she had won was now down to $200. She didn't even act like it bothered her that she had just given away $600 in less than forty minutes. I am sure it was because the worker came back with the $1,500 to pay her for the first jackpot.

The sad part of the story is that all she wanted to do is keep playing. The right sane thing to do would have been to pack up her belongings and exit the building, but no. That's when you have to ask yourself, how much is enough?

If you take a chance involving a bet of money, shouldn't you be elated if they received any profit? Take it and run. I can tell you that the way I look at it. Even now, the fact that I am taking out the time to write this book is taking a real gamble.

When I told my son I needed to write a book to explain to all the people who are out of control, gambling away everything they have and also feeling that they have no future to look forward to, he said to me that it was a great idea.

My son said that he would type it for me.

Look around. See, there is so much more to life. Don't think that the future ends tomorrow. You have to care about more things than just fulfilling your own craving and not considering anyone else no matter what. If you see the future as bright or as an exciting adventure that we all are part of, then it will be easy to want to be a part of it.

A friend said to me once that you have to hit rock bottom before you can get back up on your feet to fix the problems that your habitual act has caused. I believe that the best cure is prevention. That applies to almost every part of life. Rather than telling the world that everything is falling apart and that you are a failure, how about saying, "I am going to keep it together," and try not to be a failure or a loser. Spend your time thinking that if you put your energy into looking at all the good things that life has to hold, you will enjoy so much more. Yes, I have been over to some type of gambling casino in the past month or so. I didn't win any extra cash those times, but I did not think of myself as a loser. See, I know that people can't be winners all the time. Like I tell my grandson, "Sweetheart, you can't always be the winner because other people like to win also. Sometimes they do. Always do your best, and that's all you can do."

That is why some things don't work out like we plan; sometimes there is another designed purpose. There is no way that a person can take chances against the normal flow of life. That will throw off the whole system.

As time is goes by day after day, week by week, more people are telling me stories about what they have seen other people doing at the different gambling places. One of the things that most talk about is how some people rub the slot machine every time they make a bet. I have seen them either rub the front of the machine or the side of it. What's interesting is the fact that they must think that this action will make the machine perform the way they want. They're taking a chance.

Yesterday was a great fall day, so I helped a friend cut down trees and sawed it all up for fire wood this winter then I helped load the truck to take it to his home and stack it outside so that it is close by to bring in the house to burn in the stove for heat. We do this job every year around this time of the year, before the weather changes. It was a great day to be out in the sun so we could enjoy the fresh air outside. While we were working, we started talking about maybe going for a gambling trip next day after we unload the wood and rested for the night.

That's when a friend asked, "Have you ever seen anybody doing crazy things when they are gambling?"

I told him yes. Just days before, I saw a lot of acts that I had never witnessed before. I watched a man playing a quarter machine. The thing that he did that I found odd was that he didn't seem to care so much about watching what the machine was doing during the function of the spinning. He was only concerned about the end results. Every time the cycle stopped, this man would spin the wheel on the slot machine; then he would turn his head to the right or the left. At first, I thought, *Is this guy actually spinning the wheels on the slot machine and making sure that he doesn't look at it?*

That is just the opposite from what most people do. They come to play the machine, and there is no question that they make sure that they are watching as the slot machine rotates. All of that is part of being involved with the game. I know that is why this man stood out so much from everyone else. When the man decided that he wasn't going to play that machine anymore, he moved to the machine next to it. He still continued with the same act of spinning the wheel on the slot machine and looking away, and he would only face the machine when the sevens, any bar, or the jackpot came up.

These three things paid money and that appeared to be the only thing that he cared about. I kept thinking that it was funny. Knowing that people are spending so much of their time doing something like that routine shows there a need to repeat an act a habit.

It has now been about a month since I started writing down my thoughts about gambling. One of the main reason that

I have taken out this time in my life to write the book is that I could see that people were getting too worked up over not having enough money to live off of. They seem to always be saying that they needed more. The fact that they only have their regular jobs, no other way to make extra cash, they are turning to gambling as a way to make the money that they need. It's great if it works out that way. But I don't believe that most people are making more money by gambling. They may win a few extra dollars, but it is not so much that they don't have to continue to go to a job.

Maybe the money can be used to fulfill the goals that they may have dreamed of—a business, an investment, whatever—and if a person puts all that time into planning these dreams, it gives you something to look forward to.

As long as I could remember, I have hoped that I was lucky enough that one day I may be able to help. I guess the one thing that I see so clearly is that wanting and caring about something else is what we are all about.

Lately I have been hearing on the TV the rates of the rooms at some casinos are dropping in price. At the end of 2008, it is hard for the everyday person to continue to gamble. No money, no jobs. Most residents of California who do take chances at betting don't even go to Nevada to play anymore. Because there are so many places that are so much closer to their homes in other states now where gambling is legal.

Really, everything has changed. The way we play on the slot machines is so different. Now, when you put your cash into a slot machine, you receive a voucher in return for your money. Some machines will pay money, but not too many of them. That's the part I miss. I liked being able to put the money into the machines, and I rather have money or coins come out of the machine when it pays you. What I really miss is being able to just walk up to a machine and put a penny, nickel, or quarter in a machine as I go by. Sometimes, all I want to do is put in that one coin as I check out slot machines a lot of time. If I could, I would pay more than one machine.

One thing that has always been funny to me is the people who walk right in the door and sit down at the first machine that they see and decide that they are going to pay. They take a seat and never leave that machine. How will they ever get a chance to win anything else when they won't even try any other machine?

So many things have changed about the way that people view gambling in 2008. Clearly, there is the fact that gambling is filling up so many hours of the day. I recently explained to a cousin the difference in just the time alone involved in taking a chance; it used to be hours.

First, you would find the machine you are going to play. You put in three coins, then pull the handle. If you hit a winning combination, the extra coins that you win fall into the tile at the bottom of the slot machine; if you want to get the coins back into dollar bills, you have to take out the time to stop playing the machine. Wait for the machine to finish paying off the winnings; then you have to get a bucket from nearby to put the money in. Now you have to pick up all the coins; then you will have to locate a cashier cage in the casino. Usually there are a few lines of people waiting to do the same thing because the cashier has to pour all the coins into a machine that is going count the money. That takes a few minutes. Then the dollars are returned to the customer. Now you are ready to start all over. The whole thing takes at least thirty minutes or more. Just having to do this action slows down how fast a person is betting.

Another fact is that the money involved isn't the same. I can remember only having $20 to spend on gambling, and with that amount, I could buy a round-trip ticket on the bus line that would transport us from California to Reno, Nevada. Once we arrived in Reno, the casino would give us $10 back on the $13 bus fare, and they give us a $3.50 food coupon. What was so unbelievable about it was that not only would the $3.50 food coupon fill you up, it would make the trip home to California more enjoyable because you wouldn't be hungry during the long ride. Most of the time, we would win some money before we returned home. Nowadays that same $20 is like having a dine; it doesn't buy you a cup of coffee or anything else. To watch people putting $20 after $20 into a slot machine and not getting anything back—yes, things have changed.

A couple of days ago, I was at the casino with a friend. We sometimes go over to get a bite after working on one of the old houses that we are trying to improve. One of the things that I noticed was that most people weren't winning too much.

I like to walk around and play a lot of different type of machines. I get a chance to see other functions of the machines and how they pay off. Plus I get to see how people react to machines. My friend pointed out to me as we passed by a section of slot machines that an elderly man was play one of the slots, and every time he pushed the button to spin the wheel, he would put his head down and say a prayer. It has always been interesting to me that some people want to mix religion and gambling. Those two don't go together; that's like mixing apples and oranges. There is something wrong in viewing this activity that way. I think *desperate* is the word. I also don't think that gambling has anything to do with God, bad or good. I love it when I see people win too. He hit sevens and two triple symbols on a quarter slot machine.

One of the problems in America I believe is that it is very hard for people to work five days a week, pay their bills, buy cars and gas that cost way too much, buy food for their families that cost way too much, invest in a home that usually cost way too much, and after all of this, because money is so tight, they can't figure out any other means to make more money. Some have chosen to work overtime at their current job. That helps some. But most people are limited; there are not a lot of places they can go to try to get that extra income that will relieve some of the pressure. So they take the chance, hoping that if they buy a lottery ticket and spend time scratching them, they will win a large amount of money. Once they find the big one, it's going to fix all financial affairs.

Spending every penny that you can get in your hand on to buy tickets isn't going to get it. First of all, if the lotto tickets had that type of return back so many more people would be buying all the ticket that they could get their hands on. I know myself that no matter how many scratcher tickets I have brought, I have never gotten any that paid me more than $100.

When the California Lottery started on the TV show, first you would have to win a $100 ticket. Then you mail the ticket to the lottery commission, and they would mail back the payment for the winning ticket. And the ticket was to then be placed in a barrel along with other $100 ticket winners. If your ticket was then picked out, you would be asked to come on the show and have a chance to spin the wheel for up to two million dollars. I was lucky enough to get the winning ticket, but my ticket must not have been picked to go on the Big Spin show, because I never got my call. I could have been a millionaire years ago.

One of the things that I know that came with the check was a check stub. That is a good thing; you always have proof of payment. Also, one of the things that I found out about winning any money in the California Lottery is if you win more than $600 on a ticket, you have to complete a form and mail it and the ticket to the lottery office to be paid. Knowing this is true, one of the questions that I have been asking people is if they are winning so much money on the scratcher tickets game, then let me see the receipt stubs that came with the checks.

When you win more than $1199 at one time on a slot machine, the employee that works in the slot machine area usually comes over to the winner and asked them for their ID so that they can compute the internal revenue service information so that the right amount of federal taxes can be paid on the winnings. Some states also have you pay state taxes on the money at the time you win the cash. This happens no matter who the winner is. Once everything is approved and they can see that there is no outstanding debt that the winner owes to the IRS, then the ID is given back to the winner, and the jackpot amount is paid. A copy or a receipt of the transaction is given to the winner. In many cases, they also ask the winner if they want their picture taken. Now that I have said this, I guess what I want to know is where are the copy of the forms that were filled out at the casinos, and let me see a picture of the big jackpots that they are winning. I have a picture from when I won, and I know a lady that has showed me several pictures of her winning many times hundreds of dollars. She is one of the luckiest people that I know. To those who claim that they are winning so much money, let's see some of the picture or facts in writing, proving the results.

One of the things that I noticed more than anything was that people don't talk about all the plans they have made to go to the casino. They don't talk about any of the playing that took place while they were in the casino. What is so different now? In the past, people used to be so excited about the idea of even going anywhere near a gambling place. They would call family and friends just to brag about the fact that they were going to the casino, and they would talk about all the things that happened and how much money they took to the casino, what type of blackjack or slot machine that they played.

Now I find it odd that not only don't they tell you about the plans to get ready but they make sure that nothing is said about the activity at all. What happened? Could it be that something changed? I know that there is no way that the people can be so involved in this obsession. And most of them are sending an unbelievable amount of money.

Some people who have retired years ago are now going and getting a small part-time job. Even when you walk into some of the department stores, you see elderly people greeting you as you enter the door. When you ask what made them go back to work, they sometimes say they do not have anything to do to fill their days, so they decided why not go out and get a job. They will have more time to talk and visit with others, plus make a few dollars. Some told me they don't want to sit around the house and spend all day eating everything and getting fat. Most say that they need extra money.

I think it goes back to the statement that I made earlier: if there is all that extra time to fill in your life, why not invest the time and energy in yourself? Maybe developing a program or something that you and your loved ones may benefit from starting. If just feeling good about yourself caring. There are so many things that the future is waiting to give us.

A friend was telling me the other day that there are bus lines that will drive you to casinos now and not charge you for the ride. They also give you a food coupon for a meal once you arrive to the gambling place. Businesses know that they can give out that little bit of money on food when customers visit; they are sure that the customers will gladly come to play and eat. Most of the time, the average person will spend at a lot more money than that, so it is a good move.

Well, today was a lucky day I guess. After I dropped off my family at the airport, I felt the urge to go to the casino. I even surprised myself; I wasn't inside the building for thirty minutes, and I had won $1,024 on a penny machine. That was perfect. Within an hour, I had won $ 2,100. Now I had more than enough money to pay for my treatments and make sure that my family and my friends and I can enjoy the rest of my vacation. I am always happy whenever I win anything, and believe me, I don't win big all the time; but when I do, I make sure that I bring the money out of the place where I won it.

When I told people about my good fortune, they all were glad for me, and then there were the ones who want some of the money. No matter how much it is. I always give money away, and as I do, I say to them, "This is lucky money."

I love tipping the change people and the cashiers. Many times I have given money to the staff that is doing the cleaning up in the area around where I am playing slots machine. That is one of the main points that I want to get across to those of us who take the chance. Keep the money; use it for the millions of things that need to be done.

Yesterday, I was visiting in Southern California, and I made arrangements to go try my luck. I didn't win very much this time. I did cash in a winning ticket for $700. and two hours later, cashed another ticket for $400. They were not mine; they belonged to the person that I was with. Even though it took money to win all this, the $1,100 was gambled away before we left the casino—gone.

See, no matter how lucky you may feel, once you get the money in your hands, you have to walk out the door with it. Because before you know it, the machine you are playing or another one will suck up every bit of the winning that it gave you and *all your own cash too.*

I also saw many people just hanging out at the casino like it was their homes. They didn't want to leave, they didn't take time out to eat, and they won't even go to the restroom. Some people were sitting around in chairs, sleeping instead of going home. They act like they can't leave the money once they gamble it all away. There were several older men talking as they were sitting by the slot machine; they were not playing the machine anymore. They were not putting any cash in it, yet they were pushing the buttons and saying something to the slot. They couldn't break the tie. People get so wrapped up in the act of playing the slot machine that they won't stop. As long as there is any money that they can get a hold of, they spend it. As long as the money lasts, the more they play. But at some time, all the money disappears. You can't outlast the casino. They have way too much money, and they also can take a break and have other workers come in and relieve them.

I have seen friends playing slot machines in shifts. One would play the machine while the other person may go and eat dinner or just take a minute to get away from playing that machine. What they are trying to do is keep the machine so that no one else can get a chance to win their jackpot or any other amount on their slot machine. The funny thing is that they can do that all they want, but at some point, they will have to leave the casino's slot machine. I think that's the part some players don't understand when they make plans to gamble.

It is entertainment.

You shouldn't think that I have to keep doing this. Some people forget everything when they are taking the chance. All of a sudden, you don't have any more money. Now what to do? Gambling until all the cash is gone is way out there. I saw more of the type of activity than anything. That can't be fun.

I could tell more stories of how people are doing all kinds of things to get money, but by now you have some idea yourself. The one thing I can say is that as long as there is any money left, they will continue to find some way to get it and use it to gamble. When there is no more money, then they stop. As soon as they can find any more money, the first thought is to run and do some type of gambling again.

The lack of money in the country is causing added pressure to everyone's life, and it affects us all. I saw on the television today that 1.9 people million have lost their jobs in 2008. Of course that will make most of them more discourage. I am not sure what they are supposed to do or where they can go to make things better in their world. Several of them will run to take a chance at gambling. They believe that they will have better luck by starting over with resumes, interviews, and learning another skill. Individuals who have been involved in trades or occupation, who have talents to work one on one with other people, still should be able to keep their jobs for now. Machines can only do so much. People still are needed for medical treatments and stuff like that.

One of the things I am concerned about is the added pressure that will be put on the medical staff, when more and more people start showing up at the hospital with depression, anger, and frustration and insist on getting help because they have lost so much in their lives. The problems won't just go away. My dream is that with whatever develops, maybe I can help those who still want something and are willing to help themselves. I can see the talents people have; if they are able to transfer that into action, they would find that extra money. Let's go for it. Life is changing fast. Maybe it's just because money is becoming a harder thing for people to get in their hands.

I was talking with some nurses today, and we shared our views about how there is no middle class any more. I told them that a good friend had told me eighteen years ago that I would live to see this very thing one day. My real luck has been having good friends to share their knowledge with me. He said he could remember the way things were in America when he first came here years ago. People from other countries have a dream that if they came here to our country, spoke the language, went to school, worked hard, and saved, they would be able live the American dream. Not now. It seems to take a lot more than that.

How many times is a person suppose to rent a place to live, pay a deposit for the housing, then pay to have everything turned on, then move out after only a short time because they are unable to keep up with the bills, destroying their credit rating, and more important is the fact that some people now don't care, no concern whatsoever. They must think that no one can see what they are doing. It is what dope addicts do. After they have used everybody for everything they can get out of people who love them, they run and hide until they can get to the next location and use up those people too. Look at all the money that is being wasted. That's one of the saddest part of the story all the money went down the tubes.

I am ready now to take a real chance at making my future better, and if these plans work out, then many people will be excited and proud of the outcome. Yesterday, I was talking to a cousin about her trip to the casino. She told me that lately she can't get any winning out of the casinos that she has been going to.

I hate it when the slot machines are so tight that you can't get any payoff at all; it is always better to get something back for money you put in them. When people decide that they want to gamble, they believe that if they risk their cash, maybe they will get something in return.

They have been talking about opening another casino up by Placerville, California. I bet that would affect the casinos in the state of Nevada a lot. Some people have never liked driving up the mountain to go gamble, so they will be very happy that they can spend their money in California or other states. It has become the normal thing for people to just drive down the road for thirty minutes to an hour and be somewhere they can be gambling near their homes.

One of the things that seem to be going on is that some men and women stop by these places and decide that they can play for hours because they don't have anything else to do, so they stay and give up all the cash they have in most cases.

Before slot machines were everywhere, people would call and visit with people just to talk just hanging out enjoying being with each other. Now when people call me, they always want to know what I am doing, but they don't share any information as to what they have been up to. And I don't believe for one minute that they haven't been doing anything.

It's the middle of December 2008, and I have been talking to so many people telling me crazy things about what people are doing all in the name of gambling. Here we all are at the end of the year, and the ones who claim that they have been working so hard my question is the money? There really is not any major event in their life that the money is being spent on like buying houses, starting business, investing in stock, saving bonds, jewelry, clothes, food, or is it all just sitting in a bank account?

I know that we all have bills, and a lot of our money is wasted on outside activities. I don't see where all money went. My son was telling me on Monday morning that he was talking to friends, and he told them that his mother was writing a book on gambling. He said that most people ask if I gamble. My son grew up watching me, my cousins, my sisters, and my own mother and their friends sitting around the table gambling.

He was letting them know that gambling and taking that chance was a normal part of life. Then my son asked the question I told him to ask, "Do you know somebody that is addicted to gambling? Have they lost their mind? Are they out of control when it comes to betting?"

Once that question is asked, you almost can't get away from the person that you were talking to because they have several stories about someone they know. It can be a mother, a daughter, a sister, a cousin, an aunt, an uncle, a friend, loved ones, a coworker, or a boss—someone that has changed so much because of the need they have to always be thinking of taking that chance and spending all the money they have to see how lucky they can be.

They say that it is like talking to a completely different person than they know or knew. Wives saying things to their mates that they would never have said to them before. Women and men are out in the street hours, days, and weeks at a time doing whatever they want to get some money to keep gambling. It's wrong to leave all the things that you love and try to replace it with taking chances all the time. Some people tell me that when they say anything about going gambling without their friend who is hooked on it, all of a sudden, the real gambler starts talking about how there is no money for that in the household; the gambler has already spent hundreds or thousands of dollars gambling, but they don't want anyone else to spend a dime. They will say things like, "I know that you don't think that we have money for you to spend or waste over there at the casino." Of course the addicted gambler more often than not has actually spent so much money. During the times when they are gambling, they have lost track of the amount; they have no idea of the total.

First, they would have to count the money they started with; let's not forget all the winnings they received from taking the chance, also any money that they get from the ones they came with and any money that they get from writing checks or getting advances from credit cards at the casino, all the trips to the ATM any cash that they can use. It's like they are in a race to get something; then all of a sudden, the red flag drops on them, and it is the end of the race. Time is up; everything is gone. They have been so involved in betting they didn't realized that they were spending so much money so fast.

That's about the time when you start to see changes take place in the personality of the addicted gambler. Women are telling their men to stay away from them at the casino; yes, they get mad at the people they say they love. It is not because the loved one has done anything to them after losing the money; the gambler has no one else to take the anger out on. He or she knows that he caused the problem and even while that anger is going on, they are thinking of a way to get some more money to take that chance again.

I can't believe that the same people who were so madly in love try their luck at the casino. They are excited. But it is surprising to see how everything changes after gambling away all the money when all the action stops. If they can't get any more money to continue playing, they seem to go into a different mold.

Men have told me stories of how they would tell their mates that they were going to go out to a topless club for the night with some friends and their mate didn't seem to mind, but if he told the mate that he was thinking about going somewhere to gamble, everything changes. The mate would start saying things like we don't have money for you to be going anywhere and gambling. Arguments start over if the subject of gambling comes up, but if he or she decides to take the other person with them to gamble, then everything changes. The gambler is so happy; then everything is fine for now.

Once the addicted person gets going on the act of gambling, they tend to forget all the important things that are going on in the world. Some of the friends being that in many cases, while people are spending so much time gambling and taking chances, they aren't taking care of the needs of the people in their lives, so the ones that feel abandoned reach out to someone else. Everyone needs to be needed and loved. I would say that a lot of new relationships develop as a result of gambling whether it is people taking chances with betting or the chances that they take getting involved with new people.

I see some of the reasons why so much money is being spent so fast. It takes time for a slot machine to do what it is designed to do. You put coins in, push a button, spin the wheel, and coins fall out if you win anything.

I can't believe how many people I saw who would not let the slot machine finish its action they would hit the spin button again real fast so that the winning coins would hurry up and be counted and added to the total credit. It is almost like they don't want to take out the time to let the machine do the job. If they would stop for a moment so that the slot machine could complete the pay-off action in the normal way, it would make the gambling performance slow down; and if you slow down how fast you are gambling, then there is no question that it would slow down how much money is being wagered in a hour. Just like you could win so much more if you make a practice of cashing out the voucher and putting them in your pocket, maybe you could try a few more dollars, and if the slot machine did not pay any more, you would stop trying on that one.

I am not sure if this way of playing is being done so that no one can really see how much a slot machine is paying off or so that when someone approaches the player, it looks like the total credit on the machine is the amount of money that was put in from a wallet or a purse. This is one way of also thinking that you aren't using all the money that you are spending.

At this point, it reminds me of what I said before. It's like pinball machine; the levers on the side and the metal balls come down the middle of the board. You keep hitting the side levers, hoping that the levers hit the ball and knock it back to the top of the game so that you can continue to play. The only problem is it doesn't matter how many time you hit the levers on the side or how fast you hit them. What is prefect is to hit the metal balls so you can keep it in play. Once the ball get though the hole past the levers then the game is over.

They are hitting the devise so fast they are not even dealing with the fact that they are winning money during this whole time. That's one of the things that really surprises me.

I am getting a lot of surprises in 2009. A friend, his brother, and I went out for the night to try our luck. Before we left for the casino, we planned to have a bite to eat first. You need to make sure that you give that to yourself. Once people get so involved with betting and playing, a lot of times people forget all about those plans; they get sidetracked, and eating becomes one of the last things that they want to do. When everything is over, they can't believe how hungry they are after, and now they want to eat. I think that it would be better to spend $10 or $20 to feed your body. By just taking out that time to relax, maybe your luck can change for the good.

We didn't win on this trip; we were only in the casino for a few hours, but in the short amount of time, we counted that we had spent about $500 or $600 between the three of us. That's when we really realized how much money was being spent taking a chance on gambling.

Watching people play is always fun; you could tell that most of them were out for a Friday night. As I walked around, I noticed that I wasn't seeing much winning by any one. I tried ten or fifteen different slot machines, but I couldn't get any of them to pay a jackpot. The people that were with me said the same thing. Next thing I saw was how the building started emptying out by one o'clock in the morning. There was hardly anyone in the place. I know that there would be so many more players if they were winning; most people would not leave the casino if they were winning.

I spoke with one of the people that I gambled with, and they were having a problem about the loss of his $300. I explained to him that once you start getting your money to gamble, you must put a limit on yourself. The more you take out of the ATM the more chances you take. It's always better to try your luck for a little while, then leave. Maybe come back and give it a go on another day.

One of the biggest things that this friend and I have been able to talk about is the fact that we are not hooked on betting all the time. We like it, and if we have time and money, we may drop by and see what we can hit on the slots. We can't do that all the time, only every once in a while is okay. We laugh about how ten years ago we would go into casinos and win buckets and buckets of quarters. That's all changed. There is no way these places can allow everyone to win like they did in the past. So many people are using gambling as a way of increasing their income. The casino would go out of business if everyone won all the time.

I have come back to California, and now I can talk about what everyone is talking about: the United States has a black president.

We hope that he will make the changes that we all need; most people believe in him. They are realizing that they would rather have some things the way they were in the past. If you just worked and put in the time for your employer, then maybe we all could have a great future. Now what they see is that no matter how hard they work, no matter how many years out of their life they devote to someone's business, the employee is getting nothing in return besides a check, and that is not enough for them to live off of. Lots of jobs are being taken away; so many people think that everything is going to be fine when they are older and they retire, but sometimes other things come along and washes that all away. What should they do then? There's a good question that needs to be answered.

Today is December 18. I had a few phone calls telling me about the huge new casino that just opened in the Placerville area of California. I said years ago that people in California were waiting for a casino to come closer to where they live. Friends have been telling me since Tuesday of this week about how nice the new gambling place was. I was telling one of them it's conversations like the ones we are having that makes me realize that some people are having issues with taking a chance and betting.

I can't believe that they were talking on a regular basis for years, but now, because it has been pointed out that there is an addiction going on with them, they decide that they won't talk about gambling at all. Well, normal-thinking people know that something is not right. I am still getting calls about the new casino in Placerville. Some of them told me they were there the first day it opened up. I am getting calls from people when they are inside of the casino, yet the ones that are having problems with the gambling habit haven't said one word about the casino even now. It's been open all week. It's all over the news on television. It is within a hundred miles of Northern California. Somebody told me that the casino is advertising that if you are a club card holder and you spend $20 to play, you will receive a chance at a drawing for a million dollars during the grand opening.

Why is it that any other time most people would be talking and laughing about how they would make plans to see when they could visit the gambling place to try their luck during a vacation? If you could pass by the place, look at it; maybe stop and get a bite to eat next week or next year if you are in the area. A lot of people know it opened up, but they didn't say one word about the casino. My point is that in the past, you couldn't get them to not talk about a new gambling casino.

All the rest of us know that the speechless ones know the new casinos are under construction, and there is no way that the new places are going up in the area where they live, and they aren't aware of it.

It is five days before Christmas 2008. What's the addicted gambler been up too? Very little communicating with anyone lately, and when they do call us, most of us will be so glad to hear from them. Whatever they say, we learn what they have been up to; and most of the time, we want to believe every word of it, hoping this time they really mean what they tell us. They usually won't bring up the subject of taking chances and betting any money, but if you ask them, they say they haven't been doing any type of gambling at all. A lot of times, they will say that they don't care about it anymore, and they are going to be better in the future or that they have changed. Another good one is to say, "I just need a fresh start." Yeah right.

If there is no habit, then why can't you say the word *gamble*? It's like the word fell out of their vocabulary. Before, the ones with habits would light up like a Christmas tree if you said a thing about gambling; now they have lock jaw.

They can't have an intelligent conversation and they don't talk about a gambling habit. I know that they don't think we understand that they haven't stopped acting the same way they had in the past.

One of the things that come to my mind is where are they right now this weekend? I know if it were me, I would be driving to the casino and enjoying the great food, seeing all the pretty lights, checking out the new surrounding, and trying to see how lucky I was. When it comes to the whole outing of going to take a chance, many people I am sure drove for a few minutes to get to a nice place where they can have fun in the location that they pick. It's beautiful to be able to enjoy the trip; it's like taking a Sunday drive after church—good stuff, they have a lot of fun. As a matter of fact those are the things that were always said years ago about taking a trip.

Not talking about the habit doesn't make it go away; there is still a need to get that issue fixed. It would be harder to go around every day acting as if I had no feelings about something and not being able to express those feelings because the feelings don't just vanish. Some stress would now develop along with other things, like keeping secrets. All of these things make the habit worse. I guess once it is out in the open, it will be obvious that the problem needs to be dealt with.

All the money being spent lets me know that most people are not finding any other way to feel their life again. I ask, Where is all the money? Did they spend it all on presents for everyone for the holiday? For someone's birthday or weddings? Now I am counting down how long it takes before the addicted person faces his or her own habit. Everyone else is going to learn to accept it and live with it. They have no choice; that is the way it is. They have to live with the unhappy facts.

I have always believed that people should take a chance, but we all have a limit. We must devote some of the time and money to other things in life than just gambling. One of the things that is so surprising to me after all this time is how many people are affected by this problem but are still frighten to speak up for themselves. They wished their loved ones and themselves will be okay. Right is right, and it will be taken care of as time goes by.

Think of the future. Plan to be doing something fun, or start dreaming of what you would like to come true in the next year. Someone said to me at least I wanted something in life, which seemed to be more than what a lot of people are doing these days. In many ways, I don't think that I am as selfish as some people, and I think that makes the difference on how I see life.

Last night I got a chance to see people at a casino and the way they gambled. When I got to the casino about eight o'clock Friday evening, it was packed; I was thinking how could so many people have so much money to spend on wagering the day after Christmas 2008?

Even now it proves my point; instead of being at home with the little ones, making the most of the moments with the children, they are hanging out, hitting that slot machine spin button in a casino.

One thing that really stood out yesterday was how fast and hard the button on the machine was being hit, and I could really see how much winning was going on or not happening. Yet the players didn't seem to care about the winning part at all. When the slot machine would go around and land on something like a pay off of 50, 300, 1500 credits or whatever, they would slam the slot machines button faster and harder. I am starting to worry about what those people are doing spending money so fast. Does the family know about all the chances they are taking with this cash? I know that they are hoping to get rich; all they know is that working for someone else isn't making them rich.

People go to work, wanting to get richer and richer. What happens when you get up every day to only make money for the other guy but then he says that he doesn't want you anymore? Then what? People begin to panic. Where do you get the money? That's when the gambling comes into play.

There are no places to go and get entertained where there are humans to talk with. When people would visit friends and family, they would talk about all the things that they had on their mind and be able to vent about whatever they needed to get off their chest. Nowadays, that isn't being done. I feel lucky even more now because I have always made sure that I talked with people whether I knew them or not, and I'm always willing to open up the door and welcome anyone into my life. I make sure that I speak to them and try to make them feel at ease, as if they can share with me anything that they might want to talk about.

Now, so many laws and rules are being changed. People only have a few places to go and enjoy some of the things that they have always done before. Like smoking and drinking. We are being told that we are not allowed to smoke in public buildings or outside of them. The casino, for example, is one of the only places that a person can go and smoke without being told that they can't. When there aren't too many places to go to let your hair down, then it becomes real easy to see why people choose to retreat to somewhere that not only can they take a chance to win some money, but they can also relax. It's a simple thing, but it does matter in people's lives. It would be interesting to count how many cigarettes were smoked during an hour by each customer as they gambled. I am sure that the smoking habit would also increase during the gambling in the casino.

Two weeks ago, I visited a gambling casino place. We were there for five hours or so. I bet a few dollars. I could not get any of the slot machine that I was playing to hit any winning amounts of cash. I saw the people I was with win money. I found out later that besides the money he started with the winning and the money taken out of the ATM machine and the checks that were written it was close to $600 spent while we were there not just $20. Why use so much money trying to win a jackpot? Also, the person won't try any other slot machine. Even when I was thinking that he had stayed at the same slot machine, he was in the place all the time. That could not have been true, but it was. Because he would have had to get up and leave his machine to go and get the other money to play with. What about going to the restroom? The funny part was that he would only take the chance with the same slot machine several people really believe just a few more dollars and a few more spins on the same machine will make it hit the big one a jackpot. If the slot machine hits two hundred coins, or any other amount, you have already been lucky. To think that the more you put in, the more you get out would be great, but it doesn't always work out that way.

With cash being so hard to come by these days, people with no jobs or no way of getting any money is really going to have problems. Where is the next money going to come from? It would make so much more sense to take the winnings if they get some they are lucky they are taking that chance they should be glad there is any pay off at all.

As time continues to go by I am now starting to hear the stories about more individuals worrying not just about the pressure of their everyday lives, but also about having no income. People keep trying their chance at luck. A lot of money is being spent on just taking that chance, and nothing else is being considered in this person's life.

And to say that I made the money back, I don't think that is happening most of the time. Money is getting tight, or there is none left. When I talked with people in the past, they bragged about gambling and how they would be hanging out, enjoying making plans.

In the last few months, I haven't been hearing anything about all the money that is being used to make bets; there are even more secrets now. Rent, house notes, water bills, lights bills—a lot of them aren't getting paid. Hours are being cut at jobs. There is only so much money to go around. Once the choice is made to not put the income where it belongs, you set yourself up for failure. Also if you gamble under those conditions, it can make an enjoyable event bad. If you want to be a winner, then be a winner who brings the money home. You will be much happier if you show the family the winnings and not have to say that you lost all the money you had.

So many jobs are being lost. Fifty-five thousand in two days. I know that more and more people will be running to gambling in hopes that they can make ends meet. As the bets are made, some people will be trying so hard to get any of the money from the casino so it will help them pay the bills. In the past six months, a lot of people are moving out of houses every couple months. They are not paying their bills when for years they normally took care of all that kind of business. Some of them expect friend and family to take care of them and pay for all the bills because they love them. They bank on the fact that people love them and that they won't want them to be homeless. To make sure that they get to continue to live the way that they always have, the gambler must decide what is more important. It is not the habit to spend all the money trying to win a jackpot all the time. It is sad to watch what the loved ones are doing to fix the mess that the addicted gambler has made because they are out of control.

Hoping to help is the hard part of this story; friends and family do not understand that no matter what they do, they won't be able to stop someone else from his or her gambling habit.

As I write about gambling, it makes me laugh. One of the reasons is the funny things that I have seen when people plan to do anything about betting their money. This is their choice. In most cases, the gambler's own greed is so out there. The gambler normally doesn't care about the thing he loved in the past. There was a time when they would save money for things or events. As some of the betting is being done, they don't think anymore about taking the money to the bank account to save for another later date.

A friend told me about a recent trip to the casino. At first, he kind of walked around trying twenty-five-cent slot machines. A quarter here and a quarter there, but he really wasn't winning too much. So he decided to check on the person that he was with. He was also playing a twenty-five-cent slot machine.

When my friend saw that the other man had already won $200 and $300, he said to him, "Are you ready to go home now? We can leave anytime you are ready. I am not doing that great so we can go any time."

"We just got here."

Every time I hear a story like that, I laugh because it just conforms what I have been saying: he is a winner. He just does not seem to feel like a winner yet and couldn't break the addicted act of playing the game. Not stopping prevents him from taking the winning out the door. At that point, he is thinking about so many other things besides the real reason he went inside the place in the beginning.

To get the money, bring it home.

Even after agreeing to stay longer, my friend said he continued to walk over to the area where the other person was playing to see how he was doing. He could tell that he was still winning, but again he wasn't ready to leave.

The longer you gamble, things will ultimately change. You either win a lot more money or start to lose. Of course you, the gambler, decide how much you lose. If you don't have any discipline, you will gamble away everything that you have as the night wears on. Both of these chance takers luck changed.

The one who wasn't winning started to get money out of the slot machines that he played, not the top jackpot on all of the ones he tried, but $50, $75, and $30, which was better than the results from earlier in the evening as he kept spending one coin at a time, not three coins at a time, in the machine he saw that the slots machines were giving him more money. He also won a big jackpot on a quarter slot machine. All the double symbols across the top of the front of this slot machine paid 2,500 coins. Most people would play all three coins, but he didn't, so he got the amount for the jackpot for one coin that was bet. It was eight hundred coins.

One of the hardest things for gamblers to understand is that if you spend three coins per spin, you will go through your money faster, and if the slot machine needs to be played for one hour and someone is putting in three coins a spin in, they run out of money in less time, like in forty-five minutes. Then that player won't be able to get the jackpot that may come up because he can't make the wager in the machine that will pay him at the end. I guess if they bet one coin each spin, they could play for one hour or two hours; then the odds are better that in the period, they could hit something, and that would allow them to be luckier. This one friend has always said that this is the best way to bet when you gamble.

I know others who can show you the winning of money because they only bet one coin at a time when they gambled, not all three coins that the slot machine required. I love the fact that he has won, and if that's what works for him or anyone else, that is great.

Back to the person that was with him. He had lost his money he brought with him, plus any of the winning he got out of the slot machine and whatever money that he could get from writing checks or credit cards or ATM It was all gone, and he did not have any more cash to play with. My friend became the big winner that night.

Also, one of the things I noticed is people who only play the same slot machine have no concern about anyone else. It doesn't matter how many hours they spend in the casino, they never come to check on the companion they were with because they won't leave their slot machine.

Today I was talking with someone about buying scratcher tickets to gamble. Many dollars are spent on them. When I first started writing I was thinking that people were winning large amounts of money on that kind of gambling, but now I know that most people never mail in a winning ticket to claim any money. If they did, I am sure that they would make a copy of the winning ticket before they sent it in to the lottery office to get their payment.

I know that some people keep saying that they are winning on them. Years have gone by, and not one person has showed me a winner on those types of tickets. I haven't seen the check or the money six months have gone by. Not one person has shown me a big winning lottery ticket, a carbon copy of the claim form to get the winning amount. What about the check stub that the winners receive when the check is mailed back to them? These are four ways to prove that there was some kind of profit.

In the past, some people claimed that they were making lots of cash off the tickets. What I know now is that they don't talk at all about the tickets that they are buying to friend or family because they don't want any of them to know the large amounts of money that they are spending taking a chance.

Watching how people are acting lately, I realized that addicted gamblers don't want other people to be aware of the fact that not only are they losing all money that they earn , they are also losing all the winning that they are getting from buying the ticket if they win.

During this visit to a casino, the thing that I saw so much of that I didn't see happen in the past is how gamblers do not engage in conversations with people surrounding them.

As much as I like talking about gambling, I know that the main reason I am putting my words on these pages is I am hoping that anyone who reads them will understand that no one is trying to put them down for the habit. All I am doing now is saying it the way I see it, and I want to make sure that those who only want to keep taking a chance know that I think that they are betting on the wrong thing. They need to put much more love and care into the reality of their lives.

I know that they are living their lives and only doing what they want with the money they can get into their hands with no regard for anyone else. The gambler has to be worried; that can't be a good feeling, and there is no way that I will ever believe that worrying doesn't make people do things that they would not normally do.

People know friends and family that have to move from their apartments and houses , and now they are having to move into someone else's home so that they do not have to pay their monthly bills; the family is doing everything to help them with their problems even now.

Rather than taking a chance, gambling away all the money that comes your way, try to think about all the happy things that you want to do later. Don't keep running from place to place and lie to family and make them believe something is different than what you really have planned. No matter how many time they take out time in their life to move you to another area and you get all set up, won't just change because of the moving to a new town. Gamblers say they won't gamble anymore, but that's not true: as soon as they get set up in the new place, they'd keep doing the same old thing. Nothing has changed.

Maybe in many ways that explains half the problem addicted gamblers have; they don't want to change. Why not stick to your word. The loved ones believe what you are telling them because they want you to be happy, but they cannot force you to love yourself. Getting up and going to all the other places, trying to make anyone think that you are going to start all over now—I can't see how that is going to happen when the other life doesn't go away. If you can change the way you view life but most people don't get to keep starting over in life. And even if a person was thinking that they are going to start their life all over, friends will be watching to see if you don't commit a mistake. All of you will be hold accountable. I can understand the need to try to make extra money. I understand the need to put money away for the times when things get harder; that time will come. Then what do you do about the lack of money?

Even with all the help that is being given to the ones with an addiction to gambling, they won't stop wagering some money on gambling.

People who are spending all the money that they can get are taking it to the next level. They make trips to the bank once or twice a week, taking out money a hundred dollars at a time or more, and boy, don't that add up fast. It causes the saving or the checking account to be short of funds. So when someone tries to get paid on a bill, there is nothing to take care of the debt. They can't, because the money that was going to be spent on those bills was being used on taking that chance.

There isn't enough for everything. You won't be able to pay bills with checks or credit cards, and later before the checks clear the banks, you take the money and go gamble, believing that when you hit the big one, you are going to pay all outstanding bills. What if you don't win? Or what if you win but don't bring the money out of the casino when you win it? When the checks arrive from the banks and you can't pay them, what will you do? Now gamblers act like they don't know how the bank system works anymore. They know that they have taken out the money to gamble with, and they are straight-up lying about what they have done with the cash.

Family and friends are going to have a problem, continuing to care and love someone that they cannot trust or believe.

As this addiction gets more and more out of control, there are going to be more and more stories about how things have taken place that don't make any sense. The good part is that the good men and women in the world will always support and help each other. In many cases, they will go out of their way to try to make the person with the gambling problem better. They will try to show them all the good things that life has to offer.

More gamblers are moving from state to state, needing to live with other friends or get smaller living arrangements, because they don't have the money to pay the bills. All of that is going on because they have decided to be reckless with the money. So much money is spent on gambling in the privacy of people's homes. We were never able to do it that way before. Thousands of dollars are going on these scratcher tickets—some two dollars, three dollars, or as high as twenty dollars apiece. There is no way that all the tickets are going to pay off winning.

If there was that many winners, then I would buy them. I know I am lucky, and all I have ever won on a game in any of the states where I paid for a ticket was $100. Sometimes I may get a free game or a ticket. I would win $2, $3, or $5. But I don't win hundreds of dollars. If I buy five of them, usually three or four of them are losers. I think that is one of the biggest problems with the game, so I still do not play the tickets like a lot of people.

Those who want to believe in gambling and buying the ticket trying to win don't want to deal with the fact that all these type of tickets can't all be winners, They may know that all of them won't pay them money, yet they still take the chance over and over and continue to buy them, hoping that they will hit something that makes it worth the gamble. It would be wonderful if that happened all the time, but there is no way that could be. None of the betting is designed to always go one way or the other. If that was the case, so many more people would invest money and take a chance at making more cash. Once the quick play slot machines came into small neighborhoods, people didn't have to drive anywhere; they now were able to get up and walk a short distance to try their luck, not only on tickets, but on slot machines. They could now be played when people with addictions can't find anything else to do. I am sure that they think, "The more money I can get my hands on, the more I can gamble."

When the time comes that loved ones would understood or realize the pain and hurt that they cause, the addicted person would stop or even slow their roll.

They would think of the other person, and because of the love that they have would be stronger than their addiction to taking the chance at waging all their income. It has become sad to see that no matter how much people are being told that behavior is destroying the foundation of the lives of those close to them, the gambler doesn't seem to get it. The only thing that is important to them is to keep betting on whatever they can bet on so that they get that their needs satisfied.

Now that I can see no improvement in the present attitude, I can't assume that the future will automatically be better. Until an addict person they have a problem, they wouldn't be able to work at making the habit go away and get their life together. Stop viewing the gambling as the only means of functioning.

With all the money lacking in the average person's household, I need to make a statement about all the families that are suffering and losing all their worldly possession. A show was on the television; a reporter was talking about all the new tent cities around the country. I really was surprise to see and hear that there were more than twenty tent cities in the Sacramento area, which is the capital of California. That is frightening.

My opinion is that gambling has a lot to do with the tent cities popping up all around towns. It is very hard to believe that all these people didn't realize that their world was starting to crumble and all those material things that they hold so dear were going out the door. I know that most of us don't want to think that our life is going to be affected by outside sources, like the stock market, and if we wish real hard, we can make the bad things just go away. If we don't face problems, it will be fixed by someone else. Well, that isn't the case. When you spend all your money trying to buy everything that you see, what else can you expect?

There has to be a breaking point; living above your means eventually will cause several problems. How can you overlook what is happening? Yet the material items in many cases are still more important, and they keep holding on to them like they are better than having a roof over your head. I don't think so. Sometimes, people can't foresee that if they don't change their life, it will continue on the same road.

This past weekend, someone went out of his way to bring me an article from a newspaper that said many people have to figure out what to do now that they have no income. In some ways, gambling is to blame. I am worried about the minds of all the ones that see all the lost in our cities across the United States. Children will have even a harder time dealing with it and getting over the feeling of not knowing where they will live, where they will be sleeping, if and when they will be eating again. All of us pretty much decide that when we have children, we will provide for their every need until they are grown or able to care for themselves. Now because the adults took a chance with the money that the whole family so dearly depends on, here we are.

It's all about taking chances so many people didn't think that all their hard work would just go down the drain like it is. Once again, I feel that some of the suffering is caused by the fact that people wanted to try their luck and didn't stop in time to keep hold of the life that so dear to them.

My friend and I went to the casino. I won $160 by spending $20 and then decided to leave and go to another gambling place. As soon as we got there, I played a slot machine that had sevens on it; a jackpot came up and paid me four hundred quarters, which totaled to $100. To cut the long story short, we played from 8:00 p.m. until 6:00 a.m., and when it was all over, the one person that was with the person telling me the story didn't have enough money to buy sandwich. In the beginning when this man left for the casino, he had $600.

I asked why he worked all month and makes almost $10,000, but then as soon as he received his paycheck, he gambles and loses everything. He answered, "Because it confirms that I am a loser. I feel like a loser, and so I am one."

The only reason that the gambling stopped after twelve hours was so that the worker could go back to work When you tell someone stories of people using all their money hoping to hit the jackpot, one thing that they don't understand is that when people win, they don't keep the money. That is the part that I really do not get.

Gamblers often don't let everyone know how many times they risk their money in a week. They also don't tell the truth about the money made during the outing. If the truth be told, being able to gamble for hours means you either have plenty of money already or you have won some amount of money while playing. Many times, when they talk to someone about what money was involved, they tell only the story that they want known. It is one of the reasons why families almost don't believe what is going on with their gambling family member. Keeping secrets has made this problem worse.

Maybe one or two people not paying attention when spending everything they earn on gambling is no big deal, but it will affect the economy if we all aren't more aware of the fact that we must save some of what we have and not use it all just to play a game. I know that it is their right to have all the fun they want, and they can take out all the time that they want to gamble. All I would like to tell them is, "Get a life!"

I have seen all kinds of new hot spots popping up in California. I can't believe how easy it is to get somewhere to gamble in this state. I know that the state is having all kinds of money problems, and making it so easy for everyone to wager their cash at a chance to get rich is one way of bringing in revenue. Those who see that opportunity to make extra money and use it for that purpose are doing a good thing. They will not be able to go to that source all the time, believing it will help them make fast cash. It will be interesting to see if having places to bet will improve the budget in any state for the future.

I know that there are people who work all the time and make sure that when they aren't working, they use that money to get some winning at the casino. With all the months that have gone by, I can see I was right. The money isn't going to Nevada anymore. It is not going across state line from California to Nevada. Many of the jobs that people from other towns came to get are gone, so the workers have to go to another city or state to find a pay check. There is enough loss of income to be able to say that I did see there was going to be more problems with money because of how people would react to not having money.

I have read many statements referring to gambling problems as being a bottomless pit. There is no question that is true. I was hoping that as time went by, it would get better. Just this week, I saw a man betting a lot of his money on a slot machine. He got the machine to hit a $100 jackpot. He then stopped playing it and ran to the cashier and cashed in the ticket. Then he ran back over to the same slot machine so he could play it again. As he put more money into this same machine, he must have felt that he needed to explain to me what he was doing. I was only standing in the area where he was gambling because I had been asked to stay and watch a machine so that no one else would come along and take out the money while the other person I was with went to the smoking area. When the lady returned, I asked her if the man been winning any money on the slot machine next to hers. She said he had won a little; he had told her that a few days earlier, he had won $800 from that very same slot machine.

He was moving around almost jumping up and down, hitting the spin button so hard like he just knew that it was going to hit a big jackpot again. I walked away and went upstairs to play for about forty or fifty minutes to try my luck. I did not win anything, so I came back to check on my friends. They let me know that it was time for another smoke break. This time, as I stood there to watch the slot machine for her, the same man wanted to tell me what he had done.

He said, "I already put $80 of the $100. I won back into the slot machine. I am not going to put all of it back in it. I am going to at least be able to take home $20 home with me." He wanted me to know what was going on with him and the fact that he was betting his money and how it was affecting him. All of a sudden, he looked over at me and said, "See, the problem I have is that I have lost $500 that I can't afford to lose."

I didn't know what to say to him. There was nothing I could do about what he was saying. The next thing I knew, he got up and pushed his chair up to the slot machine and ran over to an a.m. Then he asked a woman if she could help him get money out of the ATM. She did everything she could to help him figure out how to get the money out. I heard him say to her that he wanted to take out $140 using his credit card.

All this was none of my business, but what I could see was that no matter what this man had said to me in the beginning doesn't mean a thing anymore. He was so into the wager, the gambling, taking that chance, that he forgot everything else at that moment. He was doing whatever it took to try to get back the $500 he needed, plus the $80 and now the $140. He spent over $700 on gambling that day.

When his day is over, when he talks to other people about what went on that day at the casino, he will not tell what he did with all that money. He will say that he did everything he could to win, and he just couldn't make those slot machines to pay off. Yet the real story is that he won over and over again, but it wasn't enough for him.

I looked at the stress on his face, the depression I have seen in so many people, that look that says *What to do now?* My heart goes out to him and to all of them. I know they are working hard, and in some cases, they have saved money to be able to buy stuff they felt that they had to have. Yet they go out to gamble and forget all the things that they care so much. This trip was not a winning one for me and the people I was with. Maybe on the next visit to somewhere we will be luckier.

One of the things that I like to do is to try different spots in the state, but if they don't show me any return on my money, then I leave and check out another place. I think that is one of the reasons that make me stay ahead of everyone else when it comes to taking chances. I know that I am no better than anyone else, and there is no way that anybody can win all the time. Viewing it in another way, I don't think that once I start betting I can stop.

As spring comes and I travel, I am going to take a chance and see if my luck is any good. I don't lose my mind trying to get the big one. The most important thing of all is to make sure that I enjoy myself as I play. I know that so many times, people get so involved in the idea of gambling that they can't think of anything else. I was talking about that with my son today. I have noticed even now that most of the people I know who gamble never call or visit with you unless they are going to be gambling.

If there is a gambling issue, I do not think now that it can be controlled. Why in the world would anyone take someone to a casino knowing that a person is hooked on gambling? I know why our loved one does it: love is blind. Caring for a person helps us overlook the habit. No matter what gambler does, the other person believes that the gambler will get his or her life together. If they do that, they will see that life has so much to be happy for. Try looking at everything without only thinking about yourself.

Many times, the addicted person goes off screaming and yelling at those who have nothing to do with the decisions that are being made as to what is going to be done with the gambler's money. That is one of the things that makes me mad; I really can't say that these people are using my money to gamble, yet when they don't bring their winning home, they almost act like they hate everyone. No one told them to go and do the betting in the first place, so when it is all over and done with, nobody is going to stand still and allow them to abuse friends, family, or loved ones so that the one with the habit is satisfied. I have watched this go on, and even when others try to be patient, understand, and listen as these terrible words are being said to them, they have to be wondering what the hell is going on.

Yes, in some cases the addicted gambler has borrowed cash from those same people that he is talking down too. The funny part is when it is time to pay the money back, the gambler with the habit won't communicate with the lender. You can hear the rage in their voice. But as soon as they need more money to wager and they can't get it from anywhere else, they want to call everyone that they know and try to be nice to them so that they can make someone feel sorry for them.

One of the biggest problems at that point is the person with the habit doesn't care where the money comes from or how they get some cash. Most of the time, the person taking the chance could care less if it affects the lender's life or not. Friends don't mind loaning the money as long as they know they are going to get it back. Of course the person borrowing money always agrees to pay the loan because all they want is to get off and continue to take that chance.

I have seen all of this in the past three or four years. In the beginning, I was thinking that it was just in my mind because I didn't want to believe that anyone would act like this when it came to money or taking chances on betting.

Having lived around the suffering and the disappointment as a direct cause of the habitual gamblers and how they behave made me realize that it was not all in my head. It was a fact.

Now if the subject of gambling comes up when I am talking to people, they tell me a story of how crazy people are acting, and a lot of them ask me how this could be happening. The part I have trouble with is that the person who is doing all the betting is willing to take everything, all the money, period.

What the gambler seems to want is that the rest of us do not have anything of value. They will give away every penny to be happy or try to find happiness; they are never going to find it, like they are doing things I would think that the pressure that they have put on their lives is heavy. Now they will be working overtime in life trying to do that job. Only being concerned about the hang-up that they have for gambling put them in this position.

I was telling a friend the other day that I can't believe the words that people are using when they speak of those that they know with gambling problems. In the past, nice good statement about a person were told. Now, I hear words like *terrible* and *falling apart*; both of these words are pretty strong regarding those whom we love. The fact that the words are being used shows the anger these loved ones have developed because they do not understanding. There is something really wrong.

Someone was telling me how their ATM card had been concealed because a charge to the account that was not right a whole bank account being closed. This isn't normal for most of these type of people before they became out of control.

Hey, it's pay day, the first part of the month. There hasn't been enough time to spend all the cash yet. I would like to think that is the way it is, but in most cases, people who got money coming in will be trying their luck for this month. As they are gambling, no money is being put on the house bills when there usually would be extra cash, a 50 dollar bill or 100 dollars left in a saving account to get items during the month not keeping some money in checking or saving account at a bank, no money can lead to bank accounts being close by the bank when a customer over draw and the balance is zero and what about all the money that is owed to everyone else from months before this one? Where is that money going to come from? There is always a story that comes up when it is time for the repayment. What is going to be done now? I can see it in the faces of the people around me a lot more in the last few months that many people are suffering in silence. They are at a loss. They don't have the answer to this problem. People want to know what can they do to help those addicted to gambling stop what they are doing, and as things get worse, I can't think of anything I can tell them. I wish I know something, but so far I still don't see anything that will fix the addiction.

Men and women are going to have to stop on their own. We will not be able to do that for them. You can love them forever, but you won't be able to find their happiness.

My son told me a story about how some guy was talking to him and saying that all he thinks about lately is gambling. He tries to think about other stuff, but all that comes to mind is betting. So he goes to gamble. While I was in the process of writing this book, a lady asked me what I was writing about. I told her I was writing about gambling. She offered that she knew a friend who had a real problem with gambling. He was so out of control that he was going to have to file bankruptcy. It seems that now people are using bankruptcy as the way of avoiding paying the debts that have accrued because of the gambling habits. The bad thing is that in most cases, the person filing bankruptcy made a decision to apply for the credit cards, write the check, and use money on the credit cards. They would let them borrow money, thinking that if they could get the money, they would take a chance and try to win back all the money of theirs that they had lost in the past plus earn back any other money that they took off the cards. Knowing that they had no way of paying the bills as they made them, all they were thinking of is how to get any money to get to take that chance today.

Money is really getting tight, and people don't know what they are going to do to make it. I can see all the business closing down and For Sale signs. I find that I am more determined than ever to get the book on the market hoping that it will make some of those that I can help see that life is still good and that we must always try to be happy. Some are going to need help. I will do what I can to help just like everyone else will, but there is only so much we can do and still protect ourselves. Then maybe the ones with gambling addiction will start to value their life as they did before. I know I can't fix their life. Sometimes if you can extend a little bit of a helping hand, it can make all the difference in the world to someone.

If everyone who took a chance with their money on any kind of gambling would one time think to pool those resources, just think of the great things that we as a group could do to make life easier, but everyone wants to be a millionaire by themselves. Let's hope that this way of thinking will change as we get older, or we all are going to be in real trouble.

Over the years, when I would tell people if I make any extra money I will try to put it into something that will allow those who want to benefit from their own talents and they must believe in themselves, then it all will work out toward a good future.

This week, a person I knew allowed his gambling to cause problems in his life, and he doesn't have to tell me that is the case. Everyone can see it is happening because of the changes that are taking place; he was not paying phone bills. It may not seem like a big deal to not pay the phone bill and have it turned off, but the first thing that the friends and family can see is that something has changed and something is wrong.

See, we are back to taking that chance. No matter what doesn't get taken care of, all that is going on in this person's mind is taking that chance with that money that should go in our everyday routine. What do you tell friends and family now about why you don't have the services anymore? Why aren't you paying the same bills that you paid every month for years? Why are the services ending? Why are they not paying the bills that they made sure were paid before? It is one of two things—either you don't have the money to spend on the bills because you have gambled it all away, or you have decided that you will not pay the bill or service any longer so that you can take that money to gamble with it. Either way the gambler is causing the changes when before this would have never gone on in that household.

Don't give up on your life. Keep hanging in there, for the loved ones who keeps taking that chance of spending too much money on gambling have forgotten all of that.

Don't continue to be an enabler. As much as you want to believe what the gambler is telling you, the gambler will still say whatever it takes to be able to make you think they have given up their addiction. I am becoming one of those people who think before they talk to everyone about going to gambling. It has developed into a sore pain in the side for some they get frustrated even talking about it. I know it is painful to see the ones you care for not caring about anything but gambling.

Days ago, I went to a casino with a friend. He said to me, "I will give you $20 to play with. You can try it on one of the slot machines you like to play. If you win, you can give me my $20 back and keep the other money for you to do whatever you want with that cash."

Well, we hadn't been inside the casino fifteen minutes, and that's what I did. As soon as I won, we went with that deal. As the day and night came around, I was lucky because I won $600. I made sure that I gave him some money to pay him back, and I gave him extra just in case I may need some cash from him later on another outing.

I always love when I show someone the money that comes out of the slots machines. The best part is letting friends see that you should take it home. As we talked about the evening events and counted the money we had once we returned to the house, I could see that there was joy on my friend's face because he hadn't given away all the money in his wallet and I had come back with the winning.

One of the things I saw in the last couple days is that it has been a full moon. I don't know if that made a difference or not, but this week has been pretty lucky for me. So when a friend asked me if I wanted to take a chance again and see if we could win a little more cash, I said I would love to go. I wasn't really doing anything else that day, so why not. This is when I have to say the same rules apply; you can't take that chance and gamble every day. You can't win every day. I knew I still felt lucky, and most of the time I can win a dollar or two. About an hour after we drove into the casino, I had put $20 in the slot machine and spinned the wheel maybe five times. Next thing I knew, my slot machine showed all five of the triple symbols from top to bottom on the machine. Everyone was so surprised to see the five triple symbols, and many people came by, looking at the winning jackpot. Some of them stated that they had never seen a penny slot machine hit the top jackpot amount. The total amount was one hundred thousand pennies that total to $1,000 in cash. That was great.

I was so happy to let the jackpot stay on machine, and let it make the music sound of a payoff so that everybody could see and hear what the winning sounds like. Plus they would know that the big one comes along every once in a while. I had won again. I had people come by and tell me, "You can stop that sound of the winning music on the slot machine by just pushing the spin button again."

A lot of the people who came by the machine were so excited to see that I had hit the maximum amount on the penny machine. Several said that they had never seen that kind of payoff on a penny slot machine before. One man kept going and checking on his wife, then coming back over to where I was just to see if the slot machine would count out every penny or if the casino worker would come over and pay off part of the jackpot. After about fifteen minutes, the employee told me that the lights on the penny slot machine would not come on until after all the money was counted out. I asked if they paid off any of the jackpot anymore. She said yes, but it had to be over $2,000. The jackpot took almost an hour to pay out the total amount.

Two or three people came up to me and told me they didn't lose their money to the casino; they lost their money to me.

By saying that I won their money, it looked and sounded as if they hadn't been gambling away all the money that they could get in their hands. No, the one who comes home with the money didn't gamble away their money, and the fact is that would be my money. Not the money of the ones who spent theirs. I am not sure what that statement is about. Is it because they are not wanting to congratulate me for not wager all my money and losing it, or is it that they really do not want to admit where the money is going when they take the risk? I said before that the casino only provides a product. We are adults when we are outside of these places.

We are adults when we are inside gambling. We are still adults when we come back home.

I think that sometimes people lose track of that fact when they are so busy taking that chance. They don't think about the effects their action will cause, the reaction.

My luck has been running pretty good for a week or so, I think. I wanted see if I can win some of the money that I gave away out of my one hundred thousand pennies. I know that none of us can win all the time, but I think I can hit a few more dollars this weekend. When I talk to friends about how lucky I feel and , one thing that they say a lot is they don't think that they can win. I always tell them, "Don't say that." I believe I am going to win every time I take a chance.

One Saturday evening, my best friend and I took off to the casino to see if we could win some cash. The place was really busy for a Saturday; my friend was telling me within the first hour or so that none of the slot machines seemed to be paying any jackpot to anyone and that he had been walking all around the casino but no one was talking about winning at all. I know that I played about five or six slot machines, and I wasn't getting any payoff either.

Funny enough, he said as he checked out some of the slots, he noticed that a couple was playing a slot machine, and he could see that they were hoping so much that they could win some cash. The man was playing the machine, and the woman was holding on to her man's back and shoulder. Every time he would make a bet by spinning the wheel on the slot machine, she would massage his back like he was a prize fighter. My friend said he could almost hear her saying, "Come on, Daddy, bring home the bacon." I couldn't help but laugh when he was telling me this. There is no question that they were hoping that the man could win, and then the women can gamble too, if he wins and gives her part of the money to play with.

So much cash is being spent gambling. You can see that people are doing whatever they can, hoping and wishing that it may make something happen to improve their luck for the night. I didn't win very much money that day. I did see some people who spent a lot of money; still one of the most surprising things is how people will use so much money to take the chance, to get money when they already have plenty of money in their purse or wallet or in the bank account.

As months went by, I didn't see this gambling problem getting better; it doesn't matter if it is me observing people I know, friend and family or people that I have never seen before. There doesn't seem to be an answer or a solution that I can give to the ones who love those that have a habit won't stop gambling. Are their loved ones going to help?

Once I saw a specialist on TV talking about addiction and what causes it. One of the things that he said, which was the same thing that I have seen, is a lot of the time, loved ones of the friends and family don't realize that the way they feel about the gambler affects everyone that they love, and there is no way they want the family to be unhappy, and they want to give whatever they can to them that may make them happy. That's when you start to see what people are talking to me about so that I know that the people taking all the chances. Plus they don't seem to be happy unless they are taking that chance.

As time goes by, so many friends and loved ones are really having terrible problems with gambling. It is affecting everyone and everything in their lives. Loved ones now are seeing that they can't stop what the gambling addict is doing to be able to gamble. They are so detached by the need to gamble they don't care if it is hurting the others in their life. I know that I can't fix the emotional state of mind that is being developed by the loved ones who feel like they are at their wits' end.

When a person who has not been out of town has been to work, usually there is no proof that they have given anyone the money. I have heard stories lately about how money is being given to organizations like the Red Cross, March of Dimes, or a cancer institution. The gambler wants others to believe that they are doing what they do for a greater cause. There is no way that I believe a person who has no home, no job, no bank account, who begs for money from others, is going to give the money they lent to less unfortunate people who mean nothing to the gambler. There is no way that person should be giving anybody money; if they had half a brain, they'd know that they will not be able to give money away.

I was talking to a friend this weekend, and I was happy that I called this friend after he had been out gambling; it made me feel like all my talking had paid off. He had taken the chance of using his money, and after twelve hours of playing, he made the best decision and went home with $1,100 in cash. Over the phone, I could hear how glad he was that day. I heard the excitement he had about bringing his money back home. I told him, "It isn't how much money you have, it is about bringing back what you can." Knowing that he had gambled in some way in the last five months then spent whatever money he wanted to bet, like I said before, that's up to the gambler what amount he or she wanted to spend.

When all the chances have been taken for the night, you want to get as much of the winning out of the door as you can. When you do that, save it. You can pay bills, plan to have fun, buy some of the items that you weren't able to get when you didn't have the winnings.

It is easy to talk about the fact that people are spending so much on the gambling, but I want to also tell you the good stories of when gamblers do the right things too. It is always fun to be able to say that I got some extra time and I can go see if my luck is any good. I do many things to help others; I hope that writing this little bit of information will give some support to those who are confused with this habit; it is a reminder of the feeling they had for others. You can't believe that the only thing that matters is giving away your cash. That's all right, but I care so much more about what I want for me, my friends, and my family. There are people who make adjustments to their lives because the people they care for are addicted, and it is causing several families to have to move on; in most cases, they will be leaving the gambler to find their own way of life. Those people with this habit can move from many houses, even different cities or states, and it won't cause the habit of taking the chance to go away.

I came home yesterday, and my friend told me that he had talked to his brother, who was asking if I was out gambling because he didn't know where I was. It made me feel good when I found out that he told the brother something that I know is true. He told him that just because I have money doesn't mean that I gamble. I think of going gambling most of the time when I don't have cash; that is why I do it. If betting a dollar or so will get me more money, then it is worth my time to try. If I had all the money that I see people using to win, I wouldn't need to gamble. Sometimes when you are just out and driving around, you can see several casinos; you can take the time out to go inside. Who knows you could be lucky.

In the months that have gone by, people who are only caring about gambling aren't involved with too many other things, like talking with people and performing everyday activities they used to do for the ones that mean everything to them. I have always found it interesting that the same person is claiming that they care about others and that they are doing the wagering for that reason.

One of the things a friend has told me a few times in the last six months is that they don't want anyone telling them about how they should live or how they are supposed to be doing certain things in their life. No one can stop them from living that way. If these people are doing only what they want, then why are they so mad? They are mad at everyone all the time for no reason at all. No one is doing anything; most friends and family stay away from the one with the gambling problems. What is funny to me is that the gambler seems to be so mad that whenever they get into a conversation with someone, it ends in an argument. Don't let family or friends talk about gambling or taking a chance; it doesn't matter who is doing the talking. If the conversation is about going to the casino, then the gambler with the habit is in a good mood and will be laughing, smiling, and enjoying everything that is going on in the world. You can even see them have some feedback on the subject that is being talked about. As I have been writing this, telling what I see with some people taking chances over and over, not caring about the outcome. It is only fair to make it known that more people are complaining to me about the habitual gambling that they know of.

It's the month of August 2009, and as of this time, two or three people told friends or family that they weren't going to gamble anymore. One of them said he didn't plan on gambling for the next three or four months. Some of the reasons that a couple of them made a choice to cut out the gambling for a while is it was March and Good Friday was coming.

Relationships are falling apart as well as everything else because when the one who loves them begs them not to give all their money to gambling, no matter how many times they ask them, the gambler still does only what they want. Maybe it would be a good idea if we start looking at these people the way it is; someone is going to have to remember the things in life that are important.

It is getting to the point when I have decided what my friends need to hear from me. A good friend would tell you that no matter what the gambler is doing, it isn't anyone else's problem. The gambler is going to continue to do everything they can to show their family and friends that they are responsible for themselves, and they are taking care of all the needs in their life. They feel that because of that, they don't have to listen or do anything that anyone suggests to them, even if it is the best thing for the gambler to do.

I notice that when those with gambling on their mind all the time didn't talk about other subjects, something is wrong. I have tried to bring up topics that I think people would like to discuss, but I couldn't get them into a conversation on those issue yet. They would start talking of gambling, and they could talk for hours.

Loans are being given by loved ones to help the addicted person pay bills they owe, but instead of being glad for the support, the gambler would seem to be mad. To see that family is there for them should make them want to do the right thing and stop taking chances, leave the money in the bank account for future use, and find happiness. As the gambler keeps gambling and not talking to friends or family no one knows what is happening in each other lives, where are they, who are they with, and what are they doing when they are not with the one they say they love? Talking with many friends they say when they talk to people who gamble they just don't seem to care about anything. All of them say that they can't come up with the answer to be able to stop this action. One of the questions that keeps being asked is what are you going to do now? Some are trying to make family members understand that their habit is good and that they can give the winning to us. Well that won't be happening.

Instead of going to the bank and withdrawing all the money to take that chance and to try your luck, spend some of the money on school stuff or gifts, presents for friends. Use it to give back to those who have been there for you in the past always. Lots of money is being lost; people are saying to me that they won't be gambling anymore, but then the next time they can get any money, they do the same old tricks and run to make a bet. It is going to be hard, but loved ones are going to have to realize that the story is going to be the same. My heart goes out for them, but we have to face reality because the lies are going to be told.

Gamblers don't want to stop gambling; they don't care what they tell others. The obsession of taking a chance to win the money that they believe they need to be happy is more involved than we know. I have heard it referred to as having a monkey on their back, and he keeps pushing them to the casino or to the stores to buy more losing tickets. When you ask them what is going on in their heads? What are you thinking? Do they have any plans on getting your world together? How many years are we all going to have to put up with all the crap that comes along with your habit?

Besides having to deal with the loss of money that is going to make a difference in the amount of cash that maybe available to our offspring years from now, we must deal with those who are suffering today. I understand everything that we do will cause a definite reaction. Yes, there are days when I have to stop myself from gambling. Many times, the feelings others people have I can relate to. I'd say to myself, *Boy, I feel lucky today.* When that thought enters my mind, I have to say, *No, I have so much more I need to do the during the day.* It is more important to keep track of all the things that I need to do that have to be taken care of, not just the fact that I am not busy at that hour. I have a life, so I can't get in the car and drive somewhere to bet money all the share minutes of a day. I know it is so easy to look at the time when you are sitting around being bored and just want to gamble. I don't want anyone to think that I haven't experience that mood. It is confusing to be in that position. Family and friends of gamblers are even more confused.

The addiction isn't going to just go away. We want to hope that if we continue to talk with people that have a habit of wagering money, , they will listen to the support in our voices.

Now there are stories being told to me of friend's sister and brothers or family members that are in debt because they are only thinking of themselves. Actually, it affects so much in all our lives when this happens, and it is not taken care of by a change of action.

A friend has been talking to me and showing real concern about someone that he cared for. He realized that he is going to have to plan for a future that doesn't include this person. I know that can be hard to accept, but life will go on. This has to be the time when loved ones fell helpless especially if you are a person that like being in control of things in your own life to begin with. It becomes almost impossible to watch those who can't get it under control.

There isn't any way to make people do what you want even if it is the best solution for the person's world. Can we stop the habit? I believe anything you start, you should be able to stop, but I know sometimes it just doesn't work out that way. Gamblers must pick the right road for themselves to get the addiction back in hand. Plus there are so many other parts of our lives that we don't want to look at that are going to change because of this habit. Many of the things that were going to happen won't be taking place now mainly because the ones who only love gambling is not thinking of anyone. I almost have made up my mind that if I can do anything for my friends to make adjusting easier to the painful reality, I would do it.

June 1, 2009— There was a man standing by the driveway between the dollar store and the McDonald's restaurant. He was holding a sign in his hand. Most of the people who were going past him never stopped. The sign that he held said, "Laded Off—Anything Will Help." The part that I couldn't understand was that the police department was only a couple of blocks down the street. Any other time if you looked and someone was standing anywhere begging for money of any kind, they would been taken from the area. I am sure that one of the reasons that this wouldn't be allowed is because everyone else would want to do it too. There is no way that you can let some people beg on the street to get money or hands out from passersby.

These are starting to be the times when you just don't know what to expect. When I talk with friends and they keep telling me about the things that the people they love, my heart really goes out to them. They wanted to do all they can do to try to make the gambler's life the way it was before the habit set in. It's too late for everyone to be able to forget some of the tearful, heartless statements that were made by the one who needs to deal with their habit. I really did think that as time went by, some of the people that had been talking to me, sharing the emotional and money problems that were affecting not only them but their children, friends, and almost everyone they came in contact with, would later tell me that things had gotten better, but that never took place.

Months and years have gone past; it doesn't matter if the gambling is being done in one state or the other. I have heard stories of people saying that they have to only live in one state or another because they are happier there than another state. Most of that is a choice of wanting to be where the weather may be warmer all year long, and they can gamble there freely. In many cases, what is happening is that person isn't with the family and friends, which is odd because, before, they wanted to be with these people that they love.

Summer is final starting to show up this year. Hotter temperature now. I am getting more and more phone calls about friends checking into hotels at casinos and enjoying one or two days hanging out, seeing if they can get some of the big bucks to take home. There is a lot of money that is spent staying at any casino overnight or for a few days.

When you travel to the state of Nevada, you will be able to go to so many places to try your luck. Some of the other states have only smaller reservation-type casinos and one or two that are ran by the state. It is always fun to go to bigger casinos that have slot machines with larger pay offs. I believe that if you can go to those kinds of places, you will get a better return on the money that you risk. One of the best parts is that if you are going to wager the money, you would want to know that when the machine hits something, it is worth it. Of course that is the best result all gamblers want.

One of the drawbacks about gambling is that some of the family members that are so obsessed with the habit of fulfilling their need they are not there with the dads or the children no matter what the holiday is. When you are the head of the family, it means a lot, and you should get the credit for a job well done. As children grow up, they need the cousins, uncles, aunts, parents and grandparents, and in some cases, great-grandparents, around to pass down their love, knowledge, and stories to the younger ones so that they have some view of what life may bring their way. It is too bad that some of the loved ones have decided that they are not going to be around anymore for the little ones. Even if the gambler isn't talking to everyone or not staying in contact with friends, people won't forget them, and they will not pretend that the gamblers don't exist.

I was reading an article in the newspaper yesterday. It was saying that five cases about gambling issues were going to be reviewed for appeals by the court system to decide if a person that had wagered money was entitled to the winning on the slot machine. They hope that the Supreme Court will override the decision that the local court had made in their cases. It is kind of a funny story to me: a man had been banned from a casino; maybe he just got too upset after losing. Instead of leaving the building, when he finished playing, he punched a slot machine and broke the glass. Several security officers jumped on him to remove him from the place. Before they took him to jail, they told him that he was not to come back to this casino. I went on to read the rest of the story and why this person felt he must keep driving over to this place and going inside even if he knew that he had been banned from playing there. Once he or she had been told to not come back, why do it? This is an example of the kind of action that some people take even if they are wrong. The obsession to make the bet is so important they still do it.

I was talking with a friend after the Fourth of July. We both had noticed that no one called for the holiday. I know with so many people out of work, it is hard for most of them to be in a mood to celebrate when they are forced to deal with not having the things that they need in life. Many of the state workers in California are being made to take off three Fridays out of the month, which is 15 percent of the employee pay being taken away out of their pay, That may become a problem down the line; it could make it where they are not full-time employees any more who knows what is going to happen. I am sure that it will affect when they will be able to retire and how much of a pension they get after they are no longer working. This is one of the times that I get more concerned about people not having money because it is being cut out or because they have lower pay and the worker has no control over what is going on. The fear of not having enough money starts to be part of your thinking—that is, when gamblers decide that they will take a chance, and they will gamble even more often. Because they have won before, this is a way for them to put that money back into their house; it is a plan to get some cash. Many things will have to be figured out to make extra money.

As family fall apart, the gambler doesn't have any idea about the hurt that is inflicted on the mates and kids that they left behind. They say they don't care over and over, almost as if they believe that if they keep saying it, it will come true. I know better than that. We are going to care no matter what because we love these people. The pain is getting worse and, anger is setting in. That is another reason to say that they don't care; it makes it easier to just act like it doesn't mean anything or that they are not going to let the gambler's obsession destroy the feeling in their hearts. Loved ones will be there, and they will do whatever they can do to help when the gambler calls and needs something from them. Some people have always been the providers; they only know to be the giver, and they are going to always be there to give. Even if they could turn off their emotion toward the gambler, they would still be concerned about their well bringing. Yes, it is painful to watch the suffering. The addicted gambler has no idea what damage they are causing. In many cases they wouldn't care even if they do know. It is all about them.

As I drove around looking for a place to stop, I spotted a small casino, so my friend and I went in. I was surprise when

I got inside: it said that it was a casino yet there wasn't any slot machine, and there was only two or three employees standing around talking with each other. Dealers were waiting for customers who want to play poker. My friend said to the lady, "Is this a casino?" She told us that it wasn't a casino like most customers go to you could only play poker or blackjack. Smoking was not allowed, but drinking was okay. We both asked if there were any other casino in the neighborhood. She said there was, about twenty minutes from there and that it had slot machines in it , so we decided to drive over to that casino to try our luck.

When we got there, I could see right away that the place was completely different from the first one. One could tell mainly by the amount of cars that were in the parking lot; nowhere near that many had been at the other building. It was ten in the morning; most people should be at their jobs working, not somewhere taking a chance. This is when you can't help but ask the question, Where is all the money coming from to gamble? Dollar after dollar, are they taking it out of accounts that they shouldn't be touching? Are they getting it off credit cards? Writing checks to get cash? Unless you have a pot of gold that is endless, how can anyone keep betting all the time?

While we were at the other casino, we asked questions like, Did the state of Washington or tribal group own the casino? Did they sell liquid inside? One of the things that I told my friends as we traveled in five states was, I never remember seeing so many stores where you stop to get gas, and treats now have sign on the them saying Casino Inside.

The habit of gambling has not changed. Some of the people have almost become strangers to family members and friends. I can hear the worry in the voices of the ones that are talking to me. Now there are more phone calls just to talk asking me if I know what can be done with the loved one who is not caring about anything or anyone.

In the past when someone spent money taking a chance, no one thought it was a big deal. As a person would watch them gamble at home on the computer or in casino, they would say how lucky their friends were mainly because they had no idea how much time and money were being put on making bets. Some friends never paid any attention to what was going on with the gambling because they saw it as a regular activity that the family or friend did all the time, plus they were being told that the person was winning. Maybe they are or were winning sometimes, but as the addiction got worse, the money started disappearing; then other people could see there was something going on that they would have to talk about.

Everyone is so busy living their own lives they had not taken the time to be concerned. I guess I shouldn't be either, but it is hard to see friends confused and helpless. Many times I have done things to be around to give support if

I could, yet I can only do so much if I keep writing and sharing what is going on with the problem, who knows?

I hoped that as the years went by, maybe one of the people with the addiction to gambling might change. Now the one with the habit isn't calling, writing letters, talking, or communicating with best friend that always hung out with them. They miss the time they spent together. Loved ones get up every day and go to bed every night having to deal with the fact that they don't know what the family member is doing. Yes, there is no question that people have to be more worried if you can't find the ones you love or care for.

Also, when you know that someone is spending every amount of money that they receive in bank accounts days after getting it, never saving some of the cash to take care of other needs. I am sure that by the time the money is deposited to the bank, many loans that were given to the gambler have to be paid back first; then the person who is taking that chance will feel that they should try to win back the money that they gave to the bills. In most cases there is only so much money to use during the month once that is gone; then they would have to get money again from someone. I can't help but wonder what they say to get the money out of the lender. When they get the cash, they must think that they will be able to give it back in a short time because they will have good luck at taking a chance and they can double the money and return it to pay the loan. Having a plan like this type will keep them always wagering money and giving it out to try to stay ahead; it is hard to get out of the hole. Your money is gone before you get it. Saving is next to impossible. The obsession to make the bet takes over.

I have noticed that no one talks to the addicted person, and if they do say something, not on the subject of gambling. What happened to spending time with each other and enjoying all the good stuff that we have fun doing?

Time is moving by. Their world won't stop for months at a time while the gambler is being selfish. Start thinking of someone else besides yourself. Try to remember how much it meant to you, knowing that the father, mother, sister, brother, parent, grandparent, were safe and that no one was hurting them, knowing they are well, feeling good, enjoying everyday activity. You can see the disappointment, but just not talking is not going to get it. The more the gambler hides, the more people will realize that something is wrong. As every week goes by, what most people are hoping is that time will fix all the problems. I don't see that happening. The betting is going to continue.

Even now as the month of August comes to an end, people are only hearing from members of their family when they need money. It doesn't seem to matter that they have been told already that no more will be given to them just for them to gamble away. One of the things that they don't even know is that while the gambler is obsessed with trying to figure out how to get money out of everyone, the others of us are still having a good time enjoying the fun and sun. We go out of our way to take little trip to states near California. When you take a look at all the different kinds of gambling that we can do, it is easy to see how some people think that they will be able to get more cash out of places and that maybe it will change their life.

So many things are not being done because a lot of people don't have plans for the day, so they go gambling. One of the things I tell people all the time is how busy I am. Sometimes I have to cook, do paper work, or have other type of jobs to do; now I will have to start changing my views of everyone when it comes to the slot machine and people's ability to make the right choices. As to whether to stop playing them or keep putting more and more money in them, I don't think the people that are so involved in the fact of gambling all the time won't make any plans to do anything else. As I am working on trying to meet some goals, my time and energy are to stay in control of as much of the future so that when I get there, I have some money and peace of mind, knowing that I have at least tried to do the right thing for me, my son, my grandson, and all those I love.

We can't sit there and make no plans for yourself. Once the children are gone, you understand that you don't need as much as before. Life is much easier. I don't have to worry about giving them everything. Now I don't care about the same kinds of things that I thought I had to have when I was younger and trying to raise a family. I just don't need all the extra.

We can talk for hours about some of the folk that stopped caring about their past life. Yes, the future is a big concern for all of us, but we must not destroy any of the good things that will come up because we are so busy trying to get that pot of gold.

It is easy to keep talking and saying every day that you aren't hurting anyone, but the gambler has no idea that the pain and insecurity that is being caused. They don't want to look at what happened in the family or with friends. Their loved ones just don't know what to do now. How can they make the addicted gambler stop the obsession of betting? I wish I could make it clearer to the person who is out of control. What is everyone supposed to do now that they can't call or visit the person that they love and miss? Is there going to be any way past this? Who is going to go and try to get some help to limit the amount of money that is being used or given away? Even when I do gamble, I feel like that is not going to be the only thing in the day that I am going to be doing because as soon as I complete that act, I must do something else before I rest for the night.

At first, I wasn't going to spend too much time talking about the change in the personality of the friends and family because they are being forced to accept the changes that the addicted gambler is doing. There are many feeling that now have to be coming up, feelings that most of us would never be thinking about when it comes to addictions. No talking and saying over and over I don't care about anything that the habit is causing or not causing to happen. Before the habit started, these kinds of emotions stayed hidden. People are deeply hurting in their hearts. As the gambler with the problems keeps up the same action, he or she isn't even aware of how much others are suffering because of him or her. They need to pick a position that they are going to have in life and live with it forever. Because of the choices that he or she is making, things are falling apart. What happened to all the love and concern that everyone was giving before the obsession became more important than anything.

What did they do to deserve that kind of reaction from the gambler? How do you justify that? It is like you hate everyone, like they are mad at everyone. Why? Because of what they are doing. When we all make the decision to do whatever we want, then we can't be mad at everyone because they don't agree with what you choose to do with your money or you acting the way you are.

There is a real need for people to be able to talk with others or read any kind of information that will help them in some way with the obsession of betting and taking chances. Even now I can see that people are not talking with others. I am sure that everyone is busy now that they don't get in contact with family and friends; the conversations aren't friendly or loving, sharing concern for each other.

It has become a big thing to try to understand what is going on in the addicted gambler's mind when no one is talking, not sharing any of the views and dreams that someone has. How can anyone give out that loving feeling to one another if they do not want it? I can see that there doesn't seem to be any love. I know better than that. Most people that I talk to will tell you that after all the things that have happened including having to accept the fact that the person who was everything in their life before, family loving mates now have a personality that is almost as if it is alien. It's like saying the habit is making the person become someone different. Sisters, friends, mother, women, or men in general know that there are many things that can hurt you in the world. I won't put myself outside just to gamble, also not letting anyone be aware of where I am. It is better to stay with my current worldview. If I get so involved in using all the cash on buying the wrong stuff, it will be a problem. Many people will not be able to benefit from the things that I know. It is more important to be the giver of time than to act like the only things that matter is getting more money.

Many of the freedoms that we never put too much thought into is something that we need to be reviewed. Wanting to keep a way of life the same as before is good, but in many cases, that is not going to happen. How do people just forget the friends everyone is looking to spend time with loved ones once the addicted gambler starts calling and wanting to make plans to visit people. Maybe they can travel and shop for Thanksgiving and Christmas holidays and try to get involved with others in the family for New Year. Loved ones will all get to witness the show that they put on; in many situations, there will be people not seeing or talking to some friends for four or five months or even years. What are they going to do when they meet with each other? Will everyone decide that everything is to be forgiven? No matter what has taken place, all that time that has passed and the stories that have or haven't been told. How can people just overlook the action that have been caused by those who wanted to only think of taking all the money, giving it to a business that don't really need their money.

Hundreds of other people made sure that the bills are paid. All the needs of the casino have been paid by us all; when we gamble at them, our money helps build a newer place.

I know that with all the changes going on and money being so tight even in this state I am in, it is clearly starting to show signs of the lack of employment. The ones who still have jobs to go to are uncertain about the future source of their funds. It's wrong for most of these workers to have been there, putting in all the years of work at the job, believing that they would always be able to depend on that support being there in their lives because of what they had done spending day in and day out doing that job When they look back at the time that has gone by, we are older, we don't have all the time or energy to be out there interviewing for any other forms of work. Students who are just finishing high school are having to try harder to find any kind of a job. What are they going to do? How are they going to provide for family? Where will they find the money they need? There is no doubt that everything is going to go up in price.

Some are getting out all the stuff that they can sell, and they are learning not to buy many of the things that they remember having in the past. The Internet service, cable, home phones, even cell phone have been affected. A lot of friends have said that they are going to not pay money out for any of the things that don't mean anything. See, one of the points that all of us are going to have to watch as it unfolds is there is no cash, no money, millions will not have extra.

One of my friends is now telling me how he has to be more forgiving. My question to him is why do you have to be more forgiving when you haven't done anything? Why did he feel that he had to change in any way? He has always been so giving. I don't know what would make him say something like that except the fact that he would say anything about himself, even blaming his way of looking at things as a problem when there isn't anything that I can see that he did wrong. He has always provided for friends and family; he has been a good man. He gave most of the time to the one he knows and to the others that he encounters as he goes on his way throughout the year. Now he is putting all the pressure on him. Forcing him self to feel like now he has to give more money, more time to fix the broken wing birds (that's one of the things he said to me many times) would be a big mistake. I have told him that, but time is going to show us.

What I have learned is that no matter what you do, you can't make all the people in you life feel the way you think they should. It is harder to convince people to do what you think or live the life that you think they would be better off living. Just thinking that his way of viewing issues will always have another result than the addicted gamblers, it's always harder to convert people to do what we want, and when people are on a mention to do whatever they want only, you can't change that. The person who is out to prove their point only sees his way of handing what is on his or her mind. You can't pay to change what is taking place in their mind or life. Deciding that as soon as a problem comes up, do what you can to help, be there, and give all that you can to make the gambler feel secure. What more can you do? If I could give anything back to my friend and family, it would be most of the money that has been spent needlessly making bets. Many of us today are lucky to able to get our hand on any money. Jobs are going down the tubes fast.

As more and more time has gone by, it has shown me that no matter what I was thinking, it doesn't mean one thing, even with me watching others' friends and families. I would tell them that maybe as the newest passed or that people got busy doing the things that they did before, they will change back to a better way of using the time on the clock. We can't stop the days that are going by, how will the ones that are missing all the times when they would have been sharing good moments in their lives with the addicted person?

Last year, most people were not paying any attention to the ones that were taking the chances on gambling all the time. A sad part is that all the money was gambled. I am sure several thousands of gamblers said to themselves, "I am going to spend this money, and as I win the cash, they will be giving it to my friends, my loved ones." Well, that has not happened. After more years, the loved ones haven't gotten a dollar of the cash won. So much time went into their plan, but no money is being passed on to anyone; instead, the gamblers have been trying to take as much cash from any place that they can get it so they can keep on taking that chance. I knew that there was going to be all this kind of action going on no matter what they say at times.

Many times, people think that if they just set back and didn't say anything, never complaining to the gambler about the effects that they are having on everyone around them. It doesn't matter what town they are in; people don't know if they should be talking to the addicted person about what they are doing. Nothing is being done with each other as everyone gets older, and they start thinking of the good things they are missing. In many cases, there are broken hearts.

One Thursday afternoon, a few of my friends and I said we should go and see if we can win some money. Well, it sounds like a good idea to get away for the day or evening because so much work had been done in the past few weeks getting things together right before a party that was going to be given. There were sixty guests, and everyone had a great time. I called one of the men who were going with us to ask him if he wanted to meet the rest of us at the house, or if he wanted to just drive his own truck so that he could leave later in the night at whatever time he wanted to go home. He said that he was going to come over to have coffee before he went to the casino. We hung out at the house for an hour or so; then he said, "I guess I will leave and head on over to the casino 'cause looks like it's going to be a while before you two get ready to go."

He was right. We didn't leave for the casino for another three or four hours; we weren't in a hurry to go anywhere, so we kind of took our time. As we showed up at the place, I walked over to where the friend was playing. I knew where to look for him because he always likes to try his luck and put his money into the same slot machines; they are the only machines that play. There are so many others that he can take a chance on, but for some reason, he doesn't seem to understand that fact until later when he is back in his truck going home that he could have tried other slots.

He was doing very good. Luck was on his side. He asked me right away to go to the voucher cash machine or to the cashier and get some money for him. He had gotten three cash vouchers out of the slot machine he had been playing, and he had his winning voucher in his hand. I told him I would cash them in for him like I always do. The total was $307.50. I had the machine give me the money back in $20 bills; that way if he kept playing, he doesn't have to put a hundred dollar bills in the slot machine.

I gave him his money and said, "You are doing great. I am going to see if my luck is any good. Maybe I can get my slot machine to win some money too."

One of the things I noticed when I started playing was that I couldn't win any cash. I walked around and tried about five different slot machines, but I wasn't getting any of the winnings out of any of them. Sometimes you can't win.

One morning, I received a call. The person calling wanted to ask me if I got anything from the casino (giveaways), a free rooms or a free meal. I said I had not. We had talked about this a week ago. We don't get any of the free stuff that the casino gives out. We laughed about the fact that they don't mail the people free things if you haven't been over to their business.

Three days later, a friend got a call from his brother, telling him about an invitation he received in the mail. First thing was that they were giving him something free after they could see from their recorders that the gambler had used or spent an amount of cash that would allow them to give a player something for free—a meal, a room, a cup, an ashtray, or a money coupon for each week of the month.

You won't get anything mailed to you if you don't take the time to go sign up to get the reward cards that you stick into the slot machine when playing. As you play, the machine will add credits of points on the card; it is a way to get money back. Most gamblers do like to use them. They believe that the more they use the card as they bet, the more they win. I am not sure if that is true.

In the beginning, when the casino started giving the club cards out, I was also thinking, yes, maybe this was a way to get extra return on the money I spent while gambling. When others told me about the free items that they got, I remember thinking it was a great idea. Years later, I have learned that you don't really win any more jackpots because you use the cards in a machine. I have seen many times when I put the casino's card into a slot machine, I haven't won a thing during that time. so I wouldn't be able to say that using the cards are the best thing to do. Win or lose, people like the gifts that come along with having one of the cards and putting it in the slot machine during the time when they are playing.

I stopped using the one that I had gotten in the past years; it is not so much that I don't like them. By not putting them in slot machines or any other type of machine, you could be sure that no one will know that you are in the building gambling. You must give the casino your personal information in order to have one. Before, people would tell me about all the extra things that they would get in return for spending the cash and using cards in the machine; now, they aren't saying how many presents or gifts are bring given away at the casino to bring home. I think one of the reasons that many of them don't talk about all the stuff that they are bringing back to the house now is because they are not getting the things like they did. One of the things that would change that from happening is if the people that bet money and make a point of insert the club card into the top of the slot machine, as the total builds up on the card you are awarded points for the cash that you spend. Most people use the cards all the time, no matter which casino that they gamble during their visit but now they don't go to the gift shop with any credit they earn on the card, they get the free meals or free hotel rooms that they can have at a discount on while staying at the casino. Or they ask for the money in return for the points As they bet all the money it adds up to points turning them into credits that become value able By completing a form at the desk someone will check out the amount of money that has been totaled on the card you then have a choice of what you can have on the list of give away that they offer. Some of us don't like to use the cards no matter how many freebies they give.

There was a man who had a lawsuit that he had filed against a casino because the casino business would not pay off the jackpot that the man had won during a gambling trip. The jackpots the man had gotten on the slot machine was from three kinds of machines. One of the parts of the story that really got my attention was the fact that the man had been told that he was banned from this gambling place, and from what I could tell, he was going to be removed if he returned to the business to play any games. Even if the casino had said he wasn't allowed to come inside, he still showed up over and over again to take a chance at betting money in the hopes that he would win money from the casino to take home.

What is the business to do? They must have had many reasons why they told him not to come back. One of the things the lawsuit was saying was that he had won $700 and $735 out of two slot machines, and at one point, he decided that he was going to try to play another slot machine, so he put $12 into it. As he played the machine, he won the jackpot on the slot machine of $7,945. Most of the time, if you bet more cash in a slot machine, the payoff of the machine will be higher than if you only spend small amounts it isn't always the biggest jackpot when it hits something that was almost $10,000 dollars that he had won in one day. Anyway, when the casino didn't want to pay the man the money he had won, the man couldn't do anything else but go to court. The part that is interesting to me is what would make anyone think that if they have been requested not to enter a building, what in the world would make them insist on going to the casino again?

Well, I guess the answer is the habit of gambling. That is one of the positions that people put themselves into that I would avoid. If you do that kind of stuff, the owner of the business or the worker at the place will have to decide to take the next step; they must do something to prevent the obsession. All these businesses have laws and rules that everyone must follow.

I want to talk about a recent visit to a casino. I was planning to gamble that day. I said maybe I can drive over to see if I can win some money. While the hours went by, the sun started to peek out of the clouds, and my luck was getting better—the sun melted off some of the inches of snow and ice on town streets. I asked a friend if he could drive me in his truck to the casino because a truck won't go sliding off the road from any of the ice and snow that was still everywhere. As soon as I asked that question, he refused. "I can't go over to that place anymore for now." We laughed.

I asked him, "Why did you say you can't go gambling?"

He said that he had to stay away from the casino. He said that the casino had put a hurting on him last time he was at that business. What actually took place was that a lot more money was spent on trying to win the jackpot off his favorite slot machine.

It is crazy that so many people decide that they like some kinds of machine that even if it does pay money and there isn't much of a jackpot, they still do everything they can to get to that same one to gamble on. I wish that they could see that the amount of money that they are putting into the machine hoping they will win is totaling more than the jackpot will pay off.

Truth be told, I think that the addiction to gambling has become an issue for this man like so many others. I remember talking with him years ago and explaining what I saw going on with everyone spending their money and hoping that they are going to be bring all the money home. I have gotten calls from at least five people who said they wagered money at a casino; some say that they pulled an all-nighter and didn't leave the casino for hours. They played from 8:00 p.m. until 5:00 a.m. Yes, that is gambling *for a while*. One of the things that you do realize is if someone can stay at a slot machine and keep putting dollar after dollar into the same machine, thinking that when they get all the cash they will be able to purchase all the things that they seem to want. Classic question is, why not use the money that is in your hand? Why not hold on to the money to go shopping, give the stuff that you buy to those you love or like? Most of the time, they don't have a plans at all anymore about getting gifts for family or friends. They tell that to others that they are going to give when they get paid off or are really lucky.

A friend and I dropped by a casino yesterday for about four hours. We couldn't win any money. We talked about how we were not able to have any luck at any of the gambling we tried. As I looked around the place, I could clearly see that people aren't winning; that was one of the reason the casino was so empty. I have noticed many times that if people are winning, there are a lot of people in the building because they want some money too. Maybe that's the whole point. I understand that this is the time when all of us have to decided what is more important; like I said before, this is when everyone will have to make a real decision to not just depend on possible luck all the time, which is what that habit does, and just believe in yourself.

I know it is going to be harder in the future, taking that chance, winning at gambling, that is one of the main reasons some people will have to change. If they decided to change, they will do whatever they can to get help. Let's hope that other people will be there to do all that they can to make the habit stop.

If I could give back anything to my friends and family, it would be the time and, most of all, the money that has been spent needlessly to make bets, thinking that there is no reason to save some money for a later day, like it doesn't matter anymore.

At first, I wasn't going to spend too much time talking about the changes in the personality of the friends and family because they are being forced to accept the changes that the obsessed gambler is doing that is causing all these bad feelings to start that never came up before. Saying over and over that you don't care about anything that the addicted gambler is doing or not doing is not right; before the habit started, these kinds of emotions stayed hidden.

People are hurting in their hearts even if they say it does not matter. As the gambler with the problem keeps up the same action, they aren't even aware of how much others are suffering because of them. What happened to all that love and concern?

One couple that I know gave up a lot of cash. Some of them where thinking that they were going to win because they needed to recover from all the money that they sent in December.

I once received a call from a person who asked me if I wanted to go to the casino with him and another lady. They offered to take me. It was so nice of them to include me in their planning for the day, but I had to tell him I couldn't go with them because I was already expected to be at someone home in an hour. I was going over to check if this man was all right; there had been so much snow in the last few days you have to check on the elderly. I haven't seen or talked to this person in a week or so.

Most of the time, when people win extra money, they are so happy that they make sure they call everyone they can to let them know how much money they received. When you don't get a call about it, something has happened that stopped them from getting back to you. Anyway, I still made up a care package of leftover food that we wanted him to have. We would rather give all the food that we haven't eaten to anyone who doesn't cook or can't cook for themselves. I was not able to visit too long because it started to snow. In just the thirty or forty minutes that I was in his house, the only thing that he wanted to talk about was gambling. He wanted to know if we were on the way to a casino. I said no. Maybe we would go later in the month of February. We can plan to try our luck and see if it is any good.

Many folks are being put out of their homes and losing the farms. People who always had to have all the gadgets would decide that they don't want them anymore; they stop some of the services that they had—for cable, phones, heat, food. I think that those who are gambling too much would have to pick out what they can get rid of, and they are looking at valuable items that they can sell. If they say in their minds that they don't need the stuff anymore, it will be very easy to give up or sell the belonging for money. Many are planning to leave their homes because they don't want to use any of the cash to pay the bills. Before, having all the land and the houses was so important; now, none of that make them happy. There are people that won't go a week without making a wager.

One Thursday afternoon, a friend showed up at my house. He must have smelled the catfish cooking. I told him to get a plate and help himself to everything there. While we ate and talked about making arrangements to move a few items to take them to on auction. While my guest was eating his salad and meal, he wanted to only talk of going to the casino. What was funny was that it didn't make any difference that he was supposed to be enjoying, talking, or watching a movie with the others who were in the house. I tried to talk about other subjects to get him off the goal to gamble right then. I listened to all the stories that he shared, letting me know of how it went when he was gambling over the past year or so. I couldn't get him to not talk about gambling. After he could see that the two people he was visiting were not planning on riding to the casino that afternoon, he started gathering his stuff up and went home.

One of the questions that was asked twice that night was, did I know about the luck he had in January? I told him that we don't win all the time. When I got a call from him the week after going over to the place that he liked to play at, he gave away hundreds of dollars to. During that visit, he never said a word about how much he lost that last trip. He gave them a lot of money, I think.

I talked with six people who said that we know so many things have changed about gambling, and it is hard for most people to get the money home. Previously I said that down the line, you would hear the people talking of the changes that have affected their life now that they realize all the time has done into the habitual act and they have not made any money.

I was telling a dear friend recently that we are going to start seeing several of the people that we know making big changes. One of the changes in 2010 was, people decided to move from the houses they have owned for ten or twenty years. There is no question that as all of us get older, we don't need the larger houses that we live in; we just don't need all the room when the other people are not living with you. A big house is too much work for a person alone to take care of; then you have fact that there are all the belongings in the house you do not need. What was done was they sold their things to outsiders so that they can get money. Buying cable, phones, cleaning service, cars or trucks, or anything that is of value won't be happening. Everyone knows some changes must be made so that there still is an inheritance. Then members of the whole family can attend school, college, be able to get housing and plan to have money to do the favorite parts of trips and vacation that are life changing.

It is time for all of us to start looking for some action out of each other that will make life complete. I haven't been hearing any winning stories about gambling, people are not saying anything of what they are going to do to regain the money that was wagered. Are they going to help out, working to make cash? Maybe I just don't understand; after all, I didn't think that there would ever be a point in my life when someone would tell me that if they wanted to gamble away $500 or $600 a month, it was their business, and as long as they never asked anyone for money to pay the bills that they have, no one should care how much money he or she uses to bet or how many times that they do the gambling. This is a correct statement that any person can make. What I know is that he is right: none of us have to get anyone's permission. All we have to do is decide if we care about other things anymore. What most of the ones that have become out of control only want to talk about is the idea that no matter what they do, it is okay. Some who don't have to be held accountable for their actions develop a hard way of looking at things so that they can do whatever they want, and none of us can complain.

There was a new computer-type slot machine that had been put in the casino that was forty miles away from my house. As I was checking some of the machine to see what kind of payoff I would get if I played it, I was very surprised to see two or three people sitting at one slot machine. That normally never happens. First of all, the average person always has their own slot machine that they are playing, and they don't want anyone near them when they are gambling. Many people won't even let you be around when they are betting. Mainly if you are around them, you can see what money is being won or spent.

I found out it was a one-cent slot machine. On the credit amount, there was five hundred credits in the window, or $5. Nine lines were on the counter in the front of the slot machine had been pushed so that all the payable line were covered, so that if any winning combination that come up would be paid and the number of lines that are on this machine was one, two, three, five, or ten coins. Five coins were being bet; that made it a total of forty-five pennies being bet per spin of the wheel on the slot machine.

What I couldn't believe was that a man and a woman or two women or two men were playing the same machine at the time. Men are the ones who were the money earners, so to witness two of them sharing the same five dollars on the same penny slot machine seemed odd to look at. As they played, one man would push the five pennies button, and after it would stop going into the cycle, the next man would take his turn and see if he can get the winning figures to show up in the window. There is nothing wrong with the fact that the two men are gambling at the same time together, but I know they are not usually seen playing on the same slot machine together.

While I was watching these men, what really got me was that they only had $5 to gamble. That is a small amount of money, yet they still were more interested in risking that cash for the possibility of winning some extra money. The one set of men that were sitting with each other walked all around the building to try a lot of slot machines. Sometimes they would win money off the forty-five pennies bet that they wagered. I didn't see a big jackpot come across the slot machine, but you could tell that they were having a great time as they were hitting the spin button, drinking the beers and soda, smoking, talking, and laughing with other gamblers in the area. They acted like they were having a ball. During the four hours that I was in the casino, I saw three sets of men doing the same thing—they were using one person's money and two people playing the game. Many times, I have seen several people gathered standing together cheering on one another. As they put in the coins, everyone would slap the backs and hands of each other, saying "good luck" and "congratulations" as they got the machine to pay any kind of reward. I have seen them collect money to feed in the slot machine.

I drove over to a casino in an area that I don't go too often. Maybe I have visited it once or twice before. You have to be willing to look and play all kinds of games when you are seeing that you are going to be lucky. It was fun to hear the announcement of a couple of payoffs on jackpots over the intercom. The people that I went with had a good time, just going out for the ride, seeing the sights and hearing everyone being together in the building. I guess as time goes by, we will see many changes at all casinos. There is no question that when you see the new kind of machines, the routines people perform will make them realize that something has made a difference.

While I was visiting that gambling casino on this trip, I also heard someone tell me a statement that just didn't make sense. As the slot machine was being played by a person, with a credit of 2,400 coins, he told me that the slot machine wasn't hitting any big winning combinations, but the total was adding up. Many times, the gambler was going to the ATM to withdraw cash so that he could keep on betting. I remember thinking, *You are doing great winning what you have gotten already*. I tried for six hours or so; I couldn't get any of them to pay out money. I must have played at least twenty of them, but none of them gave me back any return. I know that if that was happening to me, others who had driven over to the place can't be hitting large jackpots either.

When the man got back to the quarter slot machine, I asked him, "Are you going to keep trying the same machine?"

He turned and looked at me. "I have $16,000 on my credit card, and if I have to get it all off the card, I am going to make that damn slot machine pay."

"Please don't do that. It isn't even worth the time you are putting into playing the game. The jackpot you are playing for is lower than the amount of money that is being wagered. Your money won't be returned to you if you win."

Twenty or ten years ago, results may have been different, but in the five years that had gone by, I have seen many times when the slot machine give out less of a jackpot than the amount that people are putting in the machine. The one that he was playing paid $600 if you got four sevens in a diamond shape. That is some money, but in most cases, it won't take care of all the outstanding bills. Not too much can be done to pay back the money on cards that were gotten to gamble unless you win a large jackpot.

Money is better spent on other types of dreams. When I begin the job to talk about this habit, I did believe that everything would be taken care of as time went by. Many of the gamblers I was watching spend so much money keep saying that they were having a good time. When you look at the results of the gambling, you can see that many of them didn't own thousands of dollars. I don't know what they are going to do about all the money that they can't get back or the time that these gamblers have not spent around anyone in their lives.

How will these people get back the lost time? People are older; they are going on with their own future, meeting new friends and loved ones, starting their new families, going to college, buying homes, cars, investing time in their dreams. I know this is one of the parts of life the gambler did not plan for. As the young family member goes on with their goals, making sure that they succeed, they may forget the one who was more concerned about taking the chance and gambling away everything.

While gambling, you got to hit a good jackpot amount so that you will feel that you went in the casino to do what is smart. The more money that you can take with you, the better. Maybe you will be allowed to make loans to the ones you are gambling with, who knows? It never makes sense to play it all back. Several times when I go gambling, I watch people doing the same thing. There is no question that some of the gamblers are more involved in betting than any other thing in life. No matter what anyone does, those people will always find a way to do what they like.

I visited a casino with a friend; he was a head of the game, winning for two hours; then it was like they couldn't get the cash out of him fast enough. I told him that I wasn't winning, and anytime he wanted to go home, I was ready.

It's not that we don't love our family or friends with the need to always gamble, but they realize what I know as much as you want to make the gambler have some control and never make another bet, we can not make them stop what they are doing.

The loved ones and friends can only stand by and wait and watch. Many of the watchers are expecting some of the money that was used to gamble; they would hope to see earnings come back during the time the gambler was taking all the chances. I haven't seen the money being given to people from the gambling. I remember when it was common to say to people that if I win any money, I will give money to all the friends and family that I know. People waiting to get the money know it has not showed up. I don't think that money is being won because so many people are gambling back all the winning. If they do win cash, they won't stop satisfying their own need to play.

If the money is being used on trying to gamble and people are giving everything that they have, not really bring any of it home when they leave from gambling, then I don't see that the plans are working. But one of the statements that is made about taking that chance is how so much is going to someone besides the family or the friends.

Lately when I talked to people about how much time and money has been spent on gambling, I tell them that it is a lot. In the beginning, when they would tell me that everyone was planning to go gambling, it was not a big deal, but now people are angry, mad, and upset because they don't want to believe that all this money has gone down the drain.

There is no way to get all that money back. If the gambler keeps wagering their money, they will not be saving any of it. I think that if they win the money or jackpot from playing, the habit will make them continue with the same routine that they have for the years. They can try over and over, but it will be very hard to make up all the other money and put it back into the bank or into the pockets of those ones they took it from. If they could win all the money back, the money that they gambled for years still wouldn't be able to make those years come back that they didn't spend with people that love you. It would be nice if it all could be forgotten, but that won't happen anytime soon. Many of the friends aren't even talking to the gamblers with the habit anymore. Many people have no income. Most of them depend on the addicted gambler to make sure that they have the money. To a lot of people, financial needs are not going to be met; they will not be allowed to buy the things they want to make their dreams come true.

Let's talk about the time that isn't going to be returned to everyone's life. As people get madder, they won't go out of the way to visit the gambler, and the gambler is not putting the money aside to get together to enjoy the summer months or anytime that they would naturally be with people that they wanted to be with.

I was talking to a woman once; we shared many stories over the last ten years that I have known her. We talked about gambling. She said something to me that I do think is true: there isn't enough money to fix all the damage that has been done. The reason that is true is because everyone is starting to see that the people who are only thinking of gambling are so into what they want to do they just don't care. You can see by their action that nothing is being done. To see that the family members are not talking to the other family members is really sad and disappointing to have to live around. I am more surprised by that than anything, but it is the same type of things that most addicts do, and when you ask them where they have been or where they live, they won't answer. So you still don't know what they are doing or what is going on in their life all that time when you can't see them.

My cousin got the big jackpot in the slot machine. Hitting a jackpot for $8,000 is a good thing. I know that when the slot machine came around and landed in that payoff, it was a great feeling. My cousin said that the people who were playing in the area walked over to her and congratulated her. As excited as the players were about her hitting the jackpot on the slot machine, the gamblers had to tell her that she didn't win $8,000 on the slot. She had received the next pay line on the machine because she didn't have the total amount of money in the machine when she spun the slot machine wheel that time the fact that all the lines were covered. She won when the lucky figures came up, but she needed to spend all the money and make sure that every other amount on the machine had been pressed to get the total winning.

Sometimes we can play a slot machine for hours and you can spin it over and over, then the one time that you only risk part of the total that the slot machine requires, it will spin the winning combination on the screen. You will be paid some amount but not the biggest total on the machine. That is the time when you almost want to hit yourself for not betting all the money. You won't be able to wager the money if you don't have it to bet at the time. In most cases, people will bet the total amount on the slot machine if they can.

There has been a big gambling win, and with that is a fear factor that hadn't come into play before now. Something was stopping the person from claiming his money. What could it be? Many things can prevent you from collecting the cash, depending on the life you have been living. It's just how it goes.

One hundred thousand dollars—the gambling habit routine finally paid off taking that chance. Is it worth the risk? Here is a situation where the wager the win is what was planned from the start when the gamblers said they are going to spend money to bet. Spend some cash to fill the need that they had to play the game. I really was surprised when I heard this one, and I wanted you to know also. I believed that there was always money being used to take a chance at winning, but I had no one telling me that a person had won a large amount of cash and that the gambler was so afraid to accept the money from the winning. Knowing a lot of people would like to get some of the profits, I believe that it was lucky to know someone who won that much money. Anyone winning $100,000 is lucky. The question I always have is what will they do with all that cash? Actually many people give some of it away, but a lot of it will be gambled up again.

There is always those who can't stop the desire to take the chance, even if they know they need the money for so many other things in their lives. But they keep making a bet. Ten years ago, it was different. People acted like other parts of the future came first, and they would hold on to as much of the money as they could to pay bills, save in the bank, or make part of it for an inheritance. When people with the gambling habit make the decision to put wagering before everything else, it changes the outcome of the picture. It shows how greedy and selfish they really are.

The spring of 2010 brought a change to one of my friends' life. It was his family member who won the lucky ticket. So many things could be done with the money. It is a way of putting back some of the money that has been taken away from everyone; it is great when the gambler gets a big jackpot because one of the first things that has to be done is all the bills can be paid.

One of the things that I have been saying from the beginning is that people who continually gamble sometime do so many things to get money to gamble that they sometimes put themselves in a situation where they owe so much money to others. If and when they win a large amount of cash, they are worried that the bill collector will have their hands out first. Allowing the debts to get completely out of control, asking for help from governmental agency or private companies will have to be addressed at so point, like getting assistance for medical problems or help with food cost in the state where you live. The forms you read and sign state that if at any time you receive any extra money, you will notify the agency so that you can repay what was given to you at your time of need. If you try to cash in the big winnings to collect the money, they will try to put a lien or claim against the funds. Once the department knows, they will withdraw all the payment you owe the agency. Of course a lot of time, we sign papers without reading them totally, or we forget what we did, but the fact is still the same: you will have to pay the bill if you have the money to pay it. When we gamble, all of us hope that we will win a big amount. I have heard stories of people gambling and winning $10,000, $30,000, or as high as $50,000 and not being able to get money because of debts that they may owe to the state. I would think that it would be very hard to take the chance gambling knowing in the back of your mind that if you win more than a couple dollars, you will have to get someone else to use their ID to claim the prize.

Here we are in 2010, and I heard about someone unable to receive $100,000 winning off a lottery ticket. The action of the person doing all types of tricks to get money so that they can always gamble has caused them to not be able to get the cash when they do win a big one. Then what do you do? After you are all excited about winning, you have to start thinking of all the things that will have to be taken care of so you can collect the money. Do you owe any debts? What about the bills that keep adding up and getting more out of control? Remember the loan that you got from those around you. When you sit down and make a list of the money that you may have to pay out to cover the money owed, are you going to have cash left after giving back the money from the deal you made?

If there are no bills, then you just go to the office and collect the money from the state that you paid for the winning ticket. Before, we didn't have to think too much if there was going to be issues or problems once you won any jackpot because you pretty much knew that you would get your money. There wasn't all the electronic devices that check whatever records they have to see if there are balances that need to be paid.

The best part is that no matter how much money you win , you can place it in some kind of checking or saving account, knowing that once you find the winning numbers or ticket from any games, it is a great feeling to walk up to the deck at a store and get the proper forms to fill out, say that a payment is given to you right then while you are in the building or a check will be mailed to you in a short time.

It has got to be a terrible feeling to win and not be given the money because of fact that make you have to pay all the money out to the state of whatever other thing to cleanup the balances owed. There are many issues that can make that be the case. When that does accrue, what will you do? Did you have another way of cashing in the winning jackpot? Is there someone that you know that you can call and tell them that you got a winner? Will they be there to leave the good news in a message? Will everyone be happy because you won?

This story about a large winning payout was the first case of someone who did receive his or her winning from the state where they won the money. When you know that you can't get your money because of outstanding debts, now you have to find someone that doesn't owe money to any agency and someone whom you can trust to claim the cash for you. What type of deal will you have to make with that person? I am sure that they would not sign the ticket and claim the money unless they get something for their time and effort. The one that can't get the cash for themselves will have to agree to whatever the other person wants, or they may decide that they won't pick up the money for the one who find the winning item. And they can't have it because they would be able to use any of the money to continue the gambling habit. I don't think that most people think they can be in a situation that can stop them from going to get the money that they have won, and then all of a sudden, when they get the winning in their hands, what is the next move? I guess it is hard knowing that you are so happy about finding a winner item of any kind and wanting to tell everyone how much you won, but you can't because you have so many money problems.

Will there be those who are jealous of the accomplishment? I have heard all kinds of opinions as to what people would do and how they would handle the issue if it were them, but believe me, when it comes to telling folks about the winning of a big amount of cash, I have learned that people really surprise you with their reaction that they have to the money. I would think that everyone would want to scream out to let everyone around know that luck had come their way. Some people say that they would rather not share the information with anyone because they will feel that it is only their personal business, and they don't want others to know what is going on in the finances.

The fact that some people don't want to tell anyone that they money from gambling can have many reason that they don't want to share the knowledge with others. I can't say what makes some winner so happy that they want to tell every one that they are glad with the end results or the ones that keep quiet.

I believed that if most gamblers kept going outside sources trying to find dollar to wager, it would affect their credit rating, or something could prevent them from collecting funds. Should you keep the information to yourself? Can you call the best friends on the phone and let them know what wonderful luck they had? Are you going to have to find a friend or family members that you can depend on to speak for you? Are you going to find a person to go to the office to sign papers to get the money, use their social security number and name for any tax information that may be required? Do you have someone who will be there in your town or city to go take care of that business for you?

First, you will have to decided if you will share the facts with others. How else will they know? It is sad to have to keep the results of winning a jackpot a secret. Once you share the story with someone, you will then have to tell them what you are planning to do now that you won.

Brothers and sisters are usually close around the state you live in, and many families do have several people that they can talk to about all types of subjects. Are you going to let them pick up your winning for you? If you ask one of them to sign the forms and turn in the game winner for you, then you need to be aware of many facts before you do it. There are so many things that will change once the extra money is in play. The question that has been asked is, what will be done with the money if another person has to receive the winning for someone else?

I want to point out the real facts of winning money and the details that can cause you not to collect the cash. As time has gone by, people have told me that they know of those who couldn't get the money. Now we hope that if you have to give it away, the friendship is good and that they will be there for you giving all the money to you that you may need or want from the winning ticket. When people say they need help to get their winnings, should you go out of your way to get the money for them? Or should you stay away from the whole thing? I like the idea of not being involved with the choice that has to be made. Who is going to get the check? Will they give their information to the officials to change the taxes on their social security number?

When you wonder where the mortgage is going to come from to pay off houses so one evening as he was setting outside in the backyard of a family members house he prayed to the one that he knows is listening to him and knows his desires if you can show me the way to get these house payments paid? So I don't continue to worry and have to be stressed trying to take care of these debts. I know that he needed help, and he must have really felt that he was going to ask and hope that the wish may come true.

His wish did come true. After spending the money and purchasing the ticket, he was really lucky. Can you believe that just asking for what you want can change everything in your life? I know he had to be surprised when he saw five zeros after the first number. Most of us can buy many kinds of tickets for all types of games, but if we can get a dollar or five dollars, we are happy. Most of them are not winners. I am so happy that anyone can be lucky at this point. They will be able to take much of the money and do very positive things with the cash.

There is no question that things have changed, but there are good parts special things have been done so that something is left for the little ones. We know that everyone needs a break, and with money being so hard to come makes people glad to get any help advice or suggestions that will make their world more complete. Yes, there has been good things done, and yes, there has been some bad. Loved one friends and families who have someone in their life with gambling issues don't seem to be as close as in the past. You can tell that the people don't feel the same. I wish everything could stay the way it was, but that won't be the case.

The one who won the $100,000 has to decide what he is going to do with the jackpot. And everyone has some thought as to what they would do with the money if they were lucky and had it so they will be trying to make plans for the payoff. Just being in a position to have to think of what to do when there is money is a good place to be.

One of the sad things that had happened is jealousy. The jealousy has caused many people to say things about these winnings. Some have been disappointing, and I had to look at the person saying those remarks and wonder if the green-eyed devil was setting on his shoulder. I can't help but ask, how would they feel if they got that kind of reaction to them being lucky? Gambling is about luck, and we should still be happy if someone succeeds. I think that if the shoe was on the other foot, they would be upset and their feelings would be hurt. If they knew that someone was talking about them and putting them down when they talked to people, they would want that to stop. If the winner knew some of the statement that was said, he would be pretty surprised too. We all are going to have to realize that some people have emotions about the money that we aren't aware of. One of the reasons we are not thinking of people being mad or jealous is there is no cause for that response. No matter what amount of money is in the picture, no one should be angry. Many people can't talk about the subject of gambling without getting mad, very mad.

As time goes by, more and more people are starting to understand that they didn't think their gambling friends were so out of control. I know they want to believe it was just a thing that would pass as they got older or find another interest. Now they know that no matter how patient they are, the one that wants to gamble all the time is going to keep doing just that. The more money that comes into the household, the more the person will gamble it away.

Now I can give an example of hundreds of dollars that are still being spent by the same addicted gamblers; they are still trying to make their friends and family think that they are doing the right thing by taking any money and spending it so that they can play the game that they are in love with; it must be love because it means more to them than anything else. Even when they are with people, they don't seem to be enjoying life. All they want is to get back to the act of betting and playing those slots machines.

One question I was sure would be answered by now is, what productive thing will they do with all the winnings that they have gotten from the gambling? I am disappointed now that I can see that several people still won't give back, still only thinking of what they want and not doing anything to help others. When more time has continued to go by, nothing constructive has taken place in the lives. With all that cash the gamblers has won after three or four years, watching them not having any of the things that everyone want, shows that they have not grown as they get older not just years and age but also with our income and our belonging. When they don't do anything for the house or buy for friends or people that they work with, before they always did so that everyone knew that they were spending the money on gifts like the rest of us.

I kept looking for the large ticket items or investments into the plans or dreams for something that the rest of the family can look forward to. Several people have talked about all the plans for what they would have done with the cash. Many of them say that they would give some of the money to friends and loved ones, and they want them to put it on things that they believe they should spend the money on, items that they may need most in their lives.

Yes, a lot of people have their own opinions as to what they would do with the money if they hit a big amount on any type of jackpot. The reality is that we have so many things to use the money for that it is hard to commit giving it to what someone else might think is more important in their world.

Gambling problems have gotten worse. Some have given away so much cash, and all I have to say is that it is their life. Do they want to change their routine and try not to have the habit? Or will they continue to look at everything in the same way? Who knows, everyone would be happier if the ones with the gambling issue could see things differently, take the time to be with others, decide that they want to put more energy into that part of life. Several people have moved on and don't talk to the person who lost control of everything because they know that putting their life on hold is not going make things better. They keep watching and hoping that the friends will see them as more important than taking the chance at gambling. We cannot make them invest time in anything else including us.

Parties, housewarming, get-togethers, birthdays, and anniversary—these are the events that most people should be part of. You will not be able to do that if your head is on something else all the time. I believe that the ones who kept trying their luck when they realized that we're not getting rich that they would decide to change the fact that they were spending so much cash, but no.

We got so busy with what was happening with the money being spent that folks have lost sight of their physical and mental state. You can tell when you look at them that they are breaking down. Many of them have become so overweight that they cannot get around on their own. They have to use canes, walkers, wheelchairs, even electric type shooter machines, yet they manage to maneuver quite well in the casino. I guess you can rent them at most gambling places now while you are visiting or staying overnight.

One of the things that I didn't think I would be seeing is all the oxygen tanks being pushed along by the ones in the wheelchairs. The unbelievable thing is how many of them are smoking while they have the oxygen tube is in their nose. They do not seem to care about how dangerous it is for themselves or anyone. When the casino blows up, everyone is going to be hurt, if not killed. I think that the owners of the gambling business could not allow the smoking while using oxygen to be happening, but all they see is the customers coming in and bringing the money to gamble even if it is not safe. This is one of the issues that have changed when it comes to taking a chance. We would have never done this kind of stuff before. Now no one acts like it is a big deal.

Also there are so many people gambling who have some kind of disability. In the past, you did not see these people in the casino as much as they are now. Their health problem made them stay inside their homes. Whatever is wrong with their bodies, they figured out some way to get to the places to try their luck. Some of them not only come to play; they bring other family or friends.

Looking forward to the future, we can see that our children are growing to become men and women who are capable of planning their own lives. Some of them might be having a hard time finding jobs, which is going to make it difficult to take care of their personal needs, so they are having to depend more on other adults to let them live in their homes or apartments. In some cases, the places are so small, no more than one person should be living in them, but the parent still let them move in with them even if they may lose the housing for allowing them to be there.

In some situations, they have kids and even girlfriends or boyfriends that want to move in with them. I know it is one of those positions that nobody wants to be in, but what is the caring loved one to do when they ask or just show up to stay? They won't want them to live on the streets. I am sure that not being able to get a job may have something to do with a lack of education or work skills, and maybe part of it is because we spend way too much cash on gambling.

Even if they won money while wagering cash on any kind of betting, they are not calling and telling everyone about all the money that they had saved or all the money that they have given to others. What have they done with all the cash?

The reason you know that is because they are asking for more financial help from friends or whoever will give money to them, and they are not able to get ahead. When they can find some cash, they do the same thing. If they say they are not going to gamble, they always do if it is only to go to store and buy some kind of ticket for a lottery game.

I know people who drive to all the casinos in the outlying area where they live, writing check and trying their luck at each of the casinos. The larger amounts of money that the gamblers have won made them take more chances. Every time they would spend some of the cash; they felt it was going too fast; then they want to make that money back. I'm sure that they did win again. They may not have told anyone what the amount was, and I know it is hard on them now knowing that they had all the money from those big jackpots and to not have a dollar of it today. How sad.

The total winnings is in the thousands, but it is gone. They want to keep thinking it is still there; the facts are, it is never going to be available again. The balance has to go down if you do not stop using it. If the money is given to someone to keep, it won't be the same amount if you are always asking for the money. The jackpot will only last so long. As you tell gamblers that the money has been spent on other things, they don't want to believe it and they still want more. No one can give all of what they have to people who would gamble it rather than use it to provide for the needs of the person they are taking it from. I know that they have been told that is enough and that the money has run out and the pot is empty.

Knowing that so many people are going out now because of what they have gambled away put friends in a spot that they should not be in. They are having to let them live with them, pay their bills, feed them, and take care of their other needs, and the gambler thinks that okay. We can help for a short period of time so that they won't be living from place to place; it is always better to be able to have a roof over your head, somewhere you can lay down in a bed with peace of mind. Not having these things can cause so much stress; it is more important to think of your health and your comfort every day. It is easy to understand why gamblers are sick when they aren't involved in their habit: not eating good food and not getting the rest the body needs will sooner or later affect them. There's no doubt that they feel it happening; they know it is wrong the way they are living but they can't control their actions. Let's try to be the best we can be.

IF I HAD to say the reason for taking out the time in my
life to write this book, it would be just to let those people
that we all love know, we love you for who you are and not
for the things that you have. Remember that, and you can't
be richer.

CPSIA information can be obtained
at www.ICGtesting.com
Printed in the USA
LVOW04s0054221016
509645LV00011B/127/P